In loving memory of our friends who exemplified
the values of Bonnaroo: Emily Dunn and Jamie Wilcox,
who worked behind the scenes at Bonnaroo, and Greg
Giraldo and Michael Houser, who performed on its stages.

"Bonnaroo, as I understand it, is a state of being."
—Jim Dickinson

BONNAROO

WHAT, WHICH, THIS, THAT, THE OTHER

By Superfly Presents and AC Entertainment

Edited by Holly George-Warren

Essay by Alan Light

Photographs by Danny Clinch, C. Taylor Crothers, Morgan Harris,
Taylor Hill, Jeff Kravitz, Michael Loccisano, Adam Macchia,
Douglas Mason, Ryan Mastro, and Jason Merritt

ABRAMS IMAGE, NEW YORK

2002 • ACOUSTIC SYNDICATE • TREY ANASTASIO • BÉLA FLECK AND EDGAR MEYER • THE BIG WU • MIKE BIRBIGLIA • BLACKALICIOUS • BLIND BOYS OF ALABAMA • CAMPBELL
BAND • THE DISCO BISCUITS • DJ LOGIC • DONNA THE BUFFALO • DRUMS AND TUBA • MARK EDDIE • GABE DIXON BAND • GALACTIC • GOV'T MULE • GRAN TORINO • BEN HARPE
LIL' RASCALS BRASS BAND • LLAMA • MOE. • MOFRO • NORTH MISSISSIPPI ALLSTARS • OLD CROW MEDICINE SHOW • PARTICLE • DOTTIE PEOPLES • PHIL LESH AND FRIENDS (W
Z-TRIP • 2003 • THE ALLMAN BROTHERS BAND • ANTIBALAS AFROBEAT ORCHESTRA • BÉLA FLECK AND THE FLECKTONES (THE ORIGINAL LINEUP) • BEN HARPER AND THE IN
HOOKAH • MARK FARINA • THE FLAMING LIPS • THE FUNKY METERS • G. LOVE AND SPECIAL SAUCE • GALACTIC • GARAGE A TROIS • HACKENSAW BOYS • EMMYLOU HARRIS • WA
MONSTER GENTLEMEN • LEO KOTTKE AND MIKE GORDON • LOUQUE • THE MACHINE • MEDESKI MARTIN & WOOD • MICHAEL FRANTI AND SPEARHEAD • MIX MASTER MIKE • MOE.
LIZ PHAIR • THE POLYPHONIC SPREE • RAQ • REBIRTH BRASS BAND • JOSHUA REDMAN • RJD2 • ROBINELLA AND THE CC STRING BAND • THE ROOTS • THE SLIP • SOFT PARA
THE WAILERS • WIDESPREAD PANIC • KELLER WILLIAMS • LUCINDA WILLIAMS • JOSH WINK • YONDER MOUNTAIN STRING BAND • ZOSO • Z-TRIP • 2004 • ACOUSTIC SYNDICATE •
THE BLACK KEYS • BLUE MERLE • MARC BROUSSARD • BURNING SPEAR • BILL BURR • DAVID BYRNE • LOUIS C.K. • CALEXICO • NEKO CASE • CHRIS ROBINSON AND NEW EART
ANI DIFRANCO • BOB DYLAN • FEMI KUTI • DONAVON FRANKENREITER • GALACTIC • GOMEZ • GOV'T MULE • GRANDADDY • GUSTER • HACKENSAW BOYS • JAZZ MANDOLIN PRO
CUBANOS POSTIZOS • BONNIE MCFARLANE • NELLIE MCKAY • ERIC MCKEOWN • MEDESKI MARTIN & WOOD • MIKE DOUGHTY'S BAND • MOE. • MOFRO • MRNORTH • MY MORNING
DAMIEN RICE • ROBERT RANDOLPH AND THE FAMILY BAND • XAVIER RUDD • SAM BUSH BAND • SIMPLE KID • MINDY SMITH • SOULIVE • THE STRING CHEESE INCIDENT • TAJ M
WINWOOD • TONY WOODS • THE X-ECUTIONERS • RACHAEL YAMAGATA • YO LA TENGO • YONDER MOUNTAIN STRING BAND • 2005 • 22-20S • ALISON KRAUSS AND UNION ST
BENEVENTO-RUSSO DUO, FEATURING MIKE GORDON • THE BLACK CROWES • BLUE MERLE • BOB WEIR & RATDOG • BRAZILIAN GIRLS • JIM BREUER • BRANDI CARLILE • CITIZEN C
DONNA THE BUFFALO • DR. DOG • DRIVE-BY TRUCKERS • EARL SCRUGGS AND FRIENDS • MARK EDDIE • THE FRAMES • MARINA FRANKLIN • GABBY LA LA, FEATURING LES CL
WILL HOGE • IRON AND WINE • JOHN BUTLER TRIO • JACK JOHNSON • JURASSIC 5 • KARL DENSON'S TINY UNIVERSE • MOUSE ON MARS • CHARLIE MURPHY • MY MORNING JACKET • JOANNA NEWSOM • O.A.
ALEXANDRA MCHALE • MILE 8 • MODEST MOUSE • MOTION POTION (SAN FRANCISCO) • MOUSE ON MARS • CHARLIE MURPHY • MY MORNING JACKET • JOANNA NEWSOM • O.A.
AND CRUCIAL REGGAE • MADELINE PEYROUX • JOHN PRINE • R. B. MORRIS AND THE IRREGULARS • JOSH RITTER • RJD2 • ROSE HILL DRIVE • XAVIER RUDD • ALEXANDRA SCO
MCGEE • M. WARD • WIDESPREAD PANIC • KELLER WILLIAMS (WMD'S) • SAUL WILLIAMS • THE WORD • YONDER MOUNTAIN STRING BAND • 2006 • AMADOU AND MARIAM • AMER
THE FLECKTONES (THE ORIGINAL LINEUP) • BINDLESTIFF FAMILY CIRKUS • ANDREW BIRD • KJELL BJORGEN • BLACKALICIOUS • BLUES TRAVELER • BOJONES • BRIGHT EYES •
TALKERS • COMMON • CORN MO • MATT COSTA • CYPRESS HILL • DEADBOY AND THE ELEPHANTMEN • DEATH CAB FOR CUTIE • DEVOTCHKA • DIE NACHTIGALLEN • DIOS (MALO
ALLEN TOUSSAINT • GRAN BEL FISHER • BEN FOLDS • DAVID FORD • DONAVON FRANKENREITER • BILL FRISELL • G. LOVE AND SPECIAL SAUCE • GARAGE DELUXE • GOMEZ •
RUM • INFRADIG • I-NINE • IVAN NEVILLE'S DUMPSTAPHUNK • JD & THE STRAIGHT SHOT • SHOOTER JENNINGS • SEU JORGE • BETTYE LAVETTE • LES CLAYPOOL • LEWIS BLAC
RAMBLE DOVE • MITCH RUTMAN GROUP • MOE. • MOONSHINE STILL • ELIOT MORRIS • THE MOTET • MUTEMATH • MY MORNING JACKET • THE NEVILLE BROTHERS • NICKEL CR
RAITT • TYLER RAMSEY • REBIRTH BRASS BAND • JASPER REED • THE REFUGEE ALLSTARS OF SIERRA LEONE • RICKY SCAGGS AND KENTUCKY THUNDER • ROBERT RANDOLP
JICKS • SAMANTHA STOLLENWERCK • THE STREETS • SUPERJAM, FEATURING TREY ANASTASIO, MARCO BENEVENTO, MIKE GORDON, PHIL LESH, AND JOE RUSSO • THE WOOD BR
MCGEE • VORCZA • ABIGAIL WASHBURN • LESLIE WOODS • WORLD PARTY • ZAC BROWN BAND • 2007 • AESOP ROCK • LILY ALLEN • ANGEL AND THE LOVE MONGERS • ANNUA
BURNERS • THE BLACK ANGELS • THE BLACK KEYS • BOB WEIR & RATDOG • JOHN BOWMAN • BRAZILIAN GIRLS • JUNIOR BROWN • PIETA BROWN • T-BONE BURNETT • CAGE TH
BLACK SAINT QUARTET • DOV DAVIDOFF • THE DECEMBERISTS • ROCCO DELUCA • DIXIE DIRT • DJ SHADOW • DON BYRON PLAYS JUNIOR WALKER, FEATURING CHRIS THOMAS H
FIRECRACKER JAZZ BAND • TIM FITE • THE FLAMING LIPS • FLIGHT OF THE CONCHORDS • FOUNTAINS OF WAYNE • FRANZ FERDINAND • GALACTIC • GIRL TALK • GOGOL BOR
JESCOE • ALEXA RAY JOEL • JOHN BUTLER TRIO • KINGS OF LEON • SONYA KITCHELL • LYNNE KOPLITZ • NICK KROLL • LEWIS BLACK AND FRIENDS • THE LITTLE ONES • LOU
RADIO BEMBA SOUND SYSTEM • ZIGGY MARLEY • DEMETRI MARTIN • MICHAEL FRANTI AND SPEARHEAD • MISS LOLLY POP'S BURLESQUE COTERIE AND THE SIDESHOW BENNIE E
PAOLO NUTINI • OLD CROW MEDICINE SHOW • D. A. PENNEBAKER • THE PHILADELPHIA EXPERIMENT • BILL PLYMPTON • THE POLICE • RAILROAD EARTH • RALPH STANLEY AND
ROOTS • XAVIER RUDD • RX BANDITS • SALVADOR SANTANA BAND • SAM ROBERTS BAND • SASHA AND JOHN DIGWEED • SCOTT AMENDOLA BAND, FEATURING NELS CLINE •
HARRIS AND BLACKOUT • THE STRING CHEESE INCIDENT • STS9 • SUPERJAM, FEATURING JOHN PAUL JONES, BEN HARPER, AND AHMIR "?UESTLOVE" THOMPSON • TEA LEA
WEEN • GILLIAN WELCH • THE WESTSIDE DAREDEVILS • THE WHIGS • THE WHITE STRIPES • JOHN PAUL WHITE • WIDESPREAD PANIC • WILCO • THE WILD MAGNOLIA MARDI GRAS
ADELE • THE AFROMOTIVE • AGAINST ME! • CHARLIE ALLEN • LEO ALLEN • THE AMERICAN PLAGUE • THE AVETT BROTHERS • BACK DOOR SLAM • ERICK BAKER • BATTLES • J
MICHELLE BUTEAU • LOUIS C.K. • CARNEY • CAT POWER • CHALI 2NA • CHROMEO • COLOUR REVOLT • CORNMEAL • THE COUP • DARK STAR ORCHESTRA • DE NOVO DAHL • DEA
DJ LOGIC • DJ MEDI4 • DJ QUICKIE MART • DOCTOR OCTAGON • DRIVE-BY TRUCKERS • THE DUHKS • ELECTRIC TOUCH • THE EVERYBODYFIELDS • EXTRA GO
OBSERVATORY • GOGOL BORDELLO • JOSÉ GONZÁLEZ • ALANA GRACE • GRAND OLE PARTY • PAT GREEN • THE GREENCARDS • GRUPO FANTASMA • HARRYBU MCCAGE • HEN
JENNINGS • JACK JOHNSON • RILO KILEY • B. B. KING • TALIB KWELI • LARRY CAMPBELL, JACKIE GREENE, PHIL LESH, AND TERESA WILLIAMS • THE LEE BOYS • LES
METALLICA • MGMT • MIKE FARRIS AND THE ROSELAND RHYTHM REVUE • MINUS THE BEAR • MONEY MARK • MORNING 40 FEDERATION • MATT MORRIS • MOTION POTION (S
ORCHESTRA BAOBAB • ANDERS OSBORNE • OZOMATLI • PEARL JAM • PERSON L • PHIL LESH AND FRIENDS • PHONOGRAPH • PORTER-BATISTE-STOLTZ • BRIAN POSEHN • TH
ROYAL BANGS • SERENA RYDER • SCISSORMEN • SHARON JONES AND THE DAP-KINGS • JAKE SHIMABUKURO • SIGUR RÓS• SOJOURN • SOMETYMES WHY • SOUL REBELS B
SWORD • TEGAN AND SARA • TENNESSEE SCHMALTZ • TIËSTO • TROMBONE SHORTY & ORLEANS AVENUE • TWO GALLANTS • UMPHREY'S MCGEE • VAMPIRE WEEKEND • WALTER
JOHN MEDESKI AND KENNY WOLLESON • YONDER MOUNTAIN STRING BAND • ZAPPA PLAYS ZAPPA • 2009 • RORY ALBANESE • CHARLIE ALLEN • AMADOU AND MARIAM • AMER
OUTFIT • BEN HARPER AND RELENTLESS7 • ANDREW BIRD • THE BLACK LILLIES • MICHAEL IAN BLACK • A. A. BONDY • BON IVER • BONNAPOO 2009: TRIUMPH THE INSULT C
BRAUNOHLER • DAVID BYRNE • CAGE THE ELEPHANT • NEKO CASE • WYATT CENAC • CHAIRLIFT • CHERRYHOLMES • CITIZEN COPE • COHEED AND CAMBRIA • COMEDY CARNI
DEAR AND THE HEADLIGHTS • THE DECEMBERISTS • THE DEL MCCOURY BAND • DELTA SPIRIT • BRETT DENNEN • MADI DIAZ • ANI DIFRANCO • THE DILLINGER ESCAPE PLAN •
THE FEATURES • JIMMY FALLON • FEMI KUTI AND THE POSITIVE FORCE • FICTION FAMILY • GALACTIC • THE GIRAFFES • GIRL TALK • GOMEZ • GOV'T MULE • GRACE POTTER
HEYPENNY • HIGH ON FIRE • HOCKEY • THE HOOD INTERNET • JEDD HUGHES • ILO AND THE CORAL REEFER ALLSTARS • THE ITALS • J. BOOGIE • JETS OVERHEAD • JIMMY FA
SMAAK • NICK KROLL • KUROMA • AARON LACRATE • LEBOWSKI FEST: MOVIE PARTY • JENNY LEWIS • THE LOVELL SISTERS • THE LOW ANTHEM • THE MARS VOLTA • JESSICA
FRANCISCO) • MT. ST. HELENS VIETNAM BAND • MURS • MYNAMEISJOHNMICHAEL • THE NIKHIL KORULA BAND • NINE INCH NAILS • JULIA NUNES • PAUL OAKENFOLD • OF MON
PUBLIC ENEMY • JOE PUG • ROB RIGGLE • ROBYN HITCHCOCK AND THE VENUS 3 • RODRIGO Y GABRIELA • RUSSIAN CIRCLES • RAPHAEL SAADIQ • SANTIGOLD • KRISTEN SCH
AND THE PHARMACISTS • THOSE DARLINS • TOBACCO • TONY RICE UNIT • TOUBAB KREWE • VIEUX FARKA TOURÉ • ALLEN TOUSSAINT • TURBINE • TV ON THE RADIO • VERTIG
BAND • 2010 • AFROJACK • AGAINST ME! • TORI AMOS • JILL ANDREWS • ANGUS & JULIA STONE • AZIZ ANSARI • ATERCIOPELADOS • THE AVETT BROTHERS • B.O.B • THE BA
TRAVELER • BOMBA ESTÉREO • ALYSSA BONAGURA • BOY CRISIS • THE BRIDGE • BO BURNHAM • LEE BURRIDGE • CALEXICO • ROB CANTRELL • BRANDI CARLILE • CAROLINA
CRYSTAL METHOD (DJ SET) • KID CUDI • DAMIAN MARLEY AND NAS • DAN DEACON ENSEMBLE • DARYL HALL AND CHROMEO • DAVE MATTHEWS BAND • DAVE RAWLINGS MACH
DR. DOG • DROPKICK MURPHYS • ECLECTIC METHOD • EDWARD SHARPE AND THE MAGNETIC ZEROS • THE ENTRANCE BAND • EVEREST • FA
ANTHEM • GREG GIRALDO • THE GOSSIP • GWAR • GYPSYPHONIC DISKO • HERCULES AND LOVE AFFAIR (DJ SET) • HERE WE GO MAGIC • HOT RIZE • DANNY HOWELLS • ISIS • JO
JONATHAN TYLER AND THE NORTHERN LIGHTS • NORAH JONES • KASKADE • KINGS OF LEON • MARK KNIGHT • KRIS KRISTOFFERSON • LA RIOTS • MIRANDA LAMBERT • LC
MAYER HAWTHORNE AND THE COUNTY • JULIAN MCCULLOUGH • MEDESKI MARTIN & WOOD • THE MELVINS • MEXICAN INSTITUTE OF SOUND • MICHAEL FRANTI AND SPEARHE
FRANCISCO) • MUMFORD AND SONS • THE NATIONAL • NEEDTOBREATHE • THE NITTY GRITTY DIRT BAND • NNEKA • NEON INDIAN • NORTEC COLLECTIVE PRESENTS: BOSTIC
PUNCH BROTHERS, FEATURING CHRIS THILE • THE RBC • REBELUTION • RED CORTEZ • RISE AGAINST • JOHN ROBERTS • JOE ROBINSON • ROYAL BANGS • MARTIN SEXTON •
TEMPER TRAP • TENACIOUS D • THEY MIGHT BE GIANTS • THIEVERY CORPORATION • TINARIWEN • TINY ANIMALS • TOKYO POLICE CLUB • TROMBONE SHORTY & ORLEANS AV
BROWN BAND • 2011 • !!! • 420 COMEDY BLAZE, HOSTED BY CHEECH MARIN, FEATURING RALPHIE MAY AND THE STARS OF WORKAHOLICS • TED ALEXANDRO • ALISON KRAUSS
THE BAND OF HEATHENS • BAND OF SKULLS • NATE BARGATZE • BASSNECTAR • BEATS ANTIQUE • BEIRUT • BÉLA FLECK AND THE FLECKTONES (THE ORIGINAL LINEUP) •
AND THE FUNK UNIVERSITY • BRUCE HORNSBY AND THE NOISEMAKERS • BUFFALO SPRINGFIELD, FEATURING RICHIE FURAY, STEPHEN STILLS, NEIL YOUNG, RICK ROSAS, AND
GARY CLARK JR. • DENNIS COFFEY • COLD WAR KIDS • CORY CHISEL AND THE WANDERING SONS • ALBERTA CROSS • DÄM-FUNK AND MASTER BLAZTER • DANIEL LANOIS' BLACK
JARED DIETCH • DJ KRAZ • DJ LOGIC • DJ NEIL ARMSTRONG • DR. JOHN WITH ORIGINAL METERS AND ALLEN TOUSSAINT PERFORMING DESITIVELY BONNAROO • THE DRUMS •
FUTUREBIRDS • G. LOVE AND SPECIAL SAUCE • GALACTIC • CHILDISH GAMBINO • GIRL TALK • GIVERS • GLOBAL GYPSY PUNK REVUE, CURATED BY EUGENE HÜTZ • DONALD
HANGGAI • THE HEAD AND THE HEART • HENSON ALTERNATIVE'S STUFFED AND UNSTRUNG • INFANTREE • IRON AND WINE • J. COLE • J. RODDY WALSTON AND THE BUSINESS •
LAMONTAGNE • THE LEAGUE LIVE (PAUL SCHEER, NICK KROLL, JON LAJOIE, AND STEPHEN RANNAZZISI) • AMOS LEE • BLACK JOE LEWIS & THE HONEYBEARS • LIL WAYNE •
THE BEAUTIFUL GIRLS' MAT MCHUGH, SOLO AND ACOUSTIC • TIM MINCHIN • MINIBOONE • EUGENE MIRMAN • MISS WILLIE BROWN • MOTION POTION (SAN FRANCISCO) • MUMFO
SHAHIDAH OMAR • OPETH • PARKINGTON SISTERS • PHOSPHORESCENT • THE PIMPS OF JOYTIME • PORTUGAL. THE MAN • PRETTY LIGHTS • PRIMUS • HESTA PRYNN • RAILR
BINGHAM AND THE DEAD HORSES • SALLIE FORD AND THE SOUND OUTSIDE • SCHOOL OF SEVEN BELLS • SCISSOR SISTERS • THE SHEEPDOGS • LAUREN SHERA • SHPONGL
STS9 • SUPERJAM, FEATURING DAN AUERBACH AND DR. JOHN • THE SWORD • TRISTEN • TWIN SHADOW • UNCLE SKELETON • SHARON VAN ETTEN • WALK TH

THERS • COL. BRUCE HAMPTON AND THE CODE TALKERS • COLONEL CLAYPOOL'S BUCKET OF BERNIE BRAINS • CUT CHEMIST • THE DEL MCCOURY BAND • DIRTY DOZEN BRASS
OREY HARRIS • VIC HENLEY • JOHN BUTLER TRIO • JACK JOHNSON • NORAH JONES • JURASSIC 5 • KARL DENSON'S TINY UNIVERSE • LES CLAYPOOL'S FLYING FROG BRIGADE
OB WEIR) • RANA • SOULIVE • THE STRING CHEESE INCIDENT • AMON TOBIN • UMPHREY'S MCGEE • VINROC • WEEN • JIM WHITE • WIDESPREAD PANIC • KELLER WILLIAMS (WMD'S)
NT CRIMINALS • JAMES BROWN • BUDDAHEAD • CYRO BAPTISTA'S BEAT THE DONKEY • THE DEAD • GAVIN DEGRAW • DJ DISK • DJ SPOOKY • DRIVE-BY TRUCKERS • EKOOSTIK
HAYNES • INDECISION • JOSH KELLEY • KID KOALA • KAKI KING • BEN KWELLER • JERRY JOSEPH AND THE JACKMORMONS • JACK JOHNSON • JON CLEARY AND THE ABSOLUTE
BROWNSTONE • JASON MRAZ • MY MORNING JACKET • NEIL YOUNG AND CRAZY HORSE • THE NEW DEAL • NICKEL CREEK • NORTH MISSISSIPPI ALLSTARS • O.A.R. • PARTICLE
ONIC YOUTH • STICKY FINGERS • STS9 • TOOTS AND THE MAYTALS • TOPAZ • TORTOISE • THE TRACHTENBURG FAMILY SLIDESHOW PLAYERS • VUSI MAHLASELA OF AMANDLA!
SON GROOVE PROJECT • TED ALEXANDRO • TREY ANASTASIO • ANTIGONE RISING • THE BAD PLUS • BARBARA CUE • TODD BARRY • BILL LASWELL'S MATERIAL • MIKE BIRBIGLIA
D • CRACKER/CAMPER VAN BEETHOVEN • CUT CHEMIST AND FUNKY SOLE • DANGER MOUSE • DAVE MATTHEWS AND FRIENDS • THE DEAD • THE DEL MCCOURY BAND • DESOL
JEM • JOJO AND HIS MOJO MARDI GRAS BAND • ROBERT EARL KEEN • KINGS OF LEON • LEFTOVER SALMON • LOS LOBOS • LOS LONELY BOYS • LOUQUE • MARC RIBOT Y LOS
ET • NEW MONSOON • NORTH MISSISSIPPI ALLSTARS HILL COUNTRY REVUE • JIM NORTON • BETH ORTON • PATTI SMITH AND HER BAND • PRAXIS • PRIMUS • THE RADIATORS
• TOKYO SKA PARADISE ORCHESTRA • UMPHREY'S MCGEE • VIDA BLUE • TREY ANASTASIO • KEREN ANN • FRED ARMISEN • ASSEMBLY OF DUST • BÉLA FLECK ACOUSTIC TRIO
FEATURING JERRY DOUGLAS • THE ALLMAN BROTHERS BAND • ALO • TREY ANASTASIO • KEREN ANN • FRED ARMISEN • ASSEMBLY OF DUST • BÉLA FLECK ACOUSTIC TRIO
PETE CORREALE • TRENT DABBS • DAVE MATTHEWS BAND • DE LA SOUL • BRETT DENNEN • DISHWATER BLONDE • DJ KRUSH • DJ MEDI4 • DJ QUARTER ROY • DJ QUICKIE MART
L • GALACTIC'S KREWE DE CARNIVALE • GODFREY • THE GOURDS • GOV'T MULE • MIC HARRISON • HEARTLESS BASTARDS • VIC HENLEY • HERBIE HANCOCK'S HEADHUNTERS
• KINGS OF LEON • LAKE TROUT • RAY LAMONTAGNE • JIM LAUDERDALE • AMOS LEE • THE LEGENDARY SHACK SHAKERS • JODIE MANROSS • THE MARS VOLTA • MATISYAHU
E OLD 97'S • OLD CROW MEDICINE SHOW • OLD UNION • OLLABELLE • OUTFORMATION • OZOMATLI • PARTICLE • THE PERCEPTIONISTS • PERPETUAL GROOVE • PETER ROWAN
ECRET MACHINES • SIGNAL PATH • STEEL TRAIN • JOSS STONE • TODD STEED AND THE SONS OF PHERE • STS9 • TEA LEAF GREEN • TOOTS AND THE MAYTALS • UMPHREY'S
INOR • ARTVANDALAY • ATMOSPHERE • THE AVETT BROTHERS • BALKAN BEAT BOX • DEVENDRA BANHART • BOBBY BARE JR. • BE YOUR OWN PET • BECK • BÉLA FLECK AND
THERS PAST • GRAYSON CAPPS • THE CAT EMPIRE • CAT POWER AND THE MEMPHIS RHYTHM BAND • CLAP YOUR HANDS SAY YEAH • COL. BRUCE HAMPTON AND THE CODE
E DISCO BISCUITS • JERRY DOUGLAS • DR. JOHN • THE DRESDEN DOLLS • DUNGEN • STEVE EARLE • ELECTRIC EEL SHOCK • ELVIS COSTELLO AND THE IMPOSTERS, FEATURING
POTTER AND THE NOCTURNALS • JACKIE GREENE • BUDDY GUY • GYPSY HANDS TRIBAL BELLY DANCE • TREVOR HALL • HECTOR QIRKO BAND • VIC HENLEY • HOT BUTTERED
FRIENDS • LYRICS BORN • THE MAGIC NUMBERS • DAMIAN "JR. GONG" MARLEY • MARAH • MATISYAHU • MEDESKI MARTIN & WOOD • MIKE DOUGHTY'S BAND • MIKE GORDON AND
UG JUG • PATTON OSWALT • OYSTERHEAD • PHIL LESH AND FRIENDS • PHIL POLLARD AND HIS BAND OF HUMANS • PRESERVATION HALL JAZZ BAND • RADIOHEAD • BONNIE
FAMILY BAND • ROBINELLA • THE ROCKWELLS • RUSTED ROOT • SASHA • SON VOLT • SONIC YOUTH • SOULIVE • STEEL PULSE • STEEL TRAIN • STEPHEN MALKMUS AND THE
S, FEATURING JOHN MEDESKI AND KENNY WOLLENSON • TIM LEE BAND • TISHAMINGO • TOM PETTY AND THE HEARTBREAKERS • TORTURED SOUL • TOUBAB KREWE • UMPHREY'S
Z ANSARI • APOLLO SUNSHINE • DAVE ATTELL • BANG BANG BANG • DAVE BARNES • BEN HARPER AND THE INNOCENT CRIMINALS • DIERKS BENTLEY • BENZOS • THE BISCUIT
HANT • SAM CHAMPION • CHRISTABEL AND THE JONS • CLUTCH • COLD WAR KIDS • ORNETTE COLEMAN • DAVID CROSS • DAVID BROMBERG AND ANGEL BAND • DAVID MURRAY
OUG WAMBLE QUARTET • DR. DOG • DUBCONSCIOUS • EENORMOUS SIDECAR • EL-P • ELVIS PERKINS IN DEARLAND • PIERS FACCINI • FAVOURITE SONS • FEIST • FICTION PLANE
DSON AND DR. LONNIE SMITH QUARTET • LIONEL LOUEKE • CHARLIE LOUVIN • MAGO, FEATURING BILLY MARTIN AND JOHN MEDESKI • MANCHESTER ORCHESTRA • MANU CHAO
NCE • FINESSE MITCHELL • MUTEMATH • THE NATIONAL • THE NEW ORLEANS KLEZMER ALLSTARS • JENNIFER NICELEY • THE NIGHTWATCHMAN • NORTH MISSISSIPPI ALLSTARS
INCH MOUNTAIN BOYS • RAVI COLTRANE QUARTET • DAMIEN RICE • THE RICHARD THOMPSON BAND • ROBERT GLASPER TRIO • BRANDY ROBINSON • RODRIGO Y GABRIELA • THE
HAW • LANGHORNE SLIM • THE SLIP • JONAH SMITH • SMOKIN' DAVE AND THE PREMO DOPES • REGINA SPEKTOR • SPOON • STANTON MOORE TRIO • MAVIS STAPLES • STEFON
• TENDERHOOKS • THE DYNAMITES, FEATURING CHARLES WALKER • TIN CUP PROPHETTE • TOOL • TORTOISE • JAMES BLOOD ULMER • UNCLE EARL • MARTHA WAINWRIGHT
• KELLER WILLIAMS (WMD'S) • WOLFMOTHER • YARD DOGS ROAD SHOW • PETE YORN • 2008 • !!! • ABIGAIL WASHBURN AND THE SPARROW QUARTET, FEATURING BÉLA FLECK
AYLIN • BEAR IN HEAVEN • BIG SAM'S FUNKY NATION • THE BIG SLEEP • MIKE BIRBIGLIA • THE BLUEGRASS ALLSTARS • BOMBADIL • BROKEN SOCIAL SCENE • SOLOMON BURKE
EDERATE • DEATH CAB FOR CUTIE • DEREK TRUCKS AND SUSAN TEDESCHI SOUL STEW REVIVAL • JOE DEROSA • DIRTY DOZEN BRASS BAND • THE DISCO BISCUITS • DJ EQUAL
NEWTON FAULKNER • THE FELICE BROTHERS • THE FIERY FURNACES • BEN FOLDS • DONAVON FRANKENREITER • ZACH GALIFIANAKIS • JANEANE GAROFALO • GHOSTLAND
ER AND THE GAME BAND • HOWLIN RAIN • IRON AND WINE • ISRAEL VIBRATION • IVAN NEVILLE'S DUMPSTAPHUNK • JAKOB DYLAN AND THE GOLD MOUNTAIN REBELS • MASON
OL • LEVON HELM AND THE RAMBLE ON THE ROAD • LEZ ZEPPELIN • LITTLE FEAT • LORD T AND ELOISE • LUPE FIASCO • M.I.A. • AIMEE MANN • STEPHEN MARLEY • MASTODON
NCISCO) • MSTRKRFT • JOHN MULANEY • MY MORNING JACKET • WILLIE NELSON • NICOLE ATKINS AND THE SEA • THE NIKHIL KORULA BAND • NOMO • JIM NORTON • O.A.R.
LES • THE RACONTEURS • ROBERT PLANT AND ALISON KRAUSS, FEATURING T BONE BURNETT • ROBERT RANDOLPH'S REVIVAL • CHRIS ROCK • ROGUE WAVE • ROTARY DOWNS
ND • STATE RADIO • STEEL TRAIN • STEPHANIESID • SUPERDRAG • SUPERJAM, FEATURING KIRK HAMMETT, LES CLAYPOOL, AND EUGENE HÜTZ • THE SWELL SEASON • THE
AN" WASHINGTON • REGGIE WATTS • THE WEATHER UNDERGROUND • KANYE WEST • WHAT MADE MILWAUKEE FAMOUS • WIDESPREAD PANIC • THE WOOD BROTHERS, FEATURING
INCES • ANIMAL COLLECTIVE • AZIZ ANSARI • ZEE AVI • ERYKAH BADU • ERICK BAKER • BAND OF HORSES • BEASTIE BOYS • BÉLA FLECK AND TOUMANI DIABATE • BELLEVILLE
G, TODD BARRY, AMY SCHUMER, KUMAIL NANJIANI AND VALLEY LODGE • JIMMY BUFFETT • BOOKER T AND THE DBTS • BRUCE SPRINGSTEEN AND THE E STREET BAND • KURT
N'NAHS • THE DIRTY PROJECTORS • DIRTY SWEET • DJ QUICKIE MART • DAN DYER • JUSTIN TOWNES EARLE • ELVIS COSTELLO • ALBERTA CROSS • CRYSTAL CASTLES • DAVID GRISMAN QUINTET
RISTIAN FINNEGAN, ARJ BARKER, JANEANE GAROFALO, NICK THUNE, AND PETE HOLMES • ELVIS COSTELLO • ALBERTA CROSS • CRYSTAL CASTLES • DAVID GRISMAN QUINTET
E NOCTURNALS • AL GREEN • GRIZZLY BEAR • GYPSYPHONIC DISKO • MERLE HAGGARD • JERRY HANNAN • HEARTLESS BASTARDS • THE HEAVY PETS • DON HERTZFELDT
COTTON JONES • WAYNE FEDERMAN • KAKI KING • KATZENJAMMER • ROBERT EARL KEEN • KI: THEORY • KING SUNNY ADÉ AND THE AFRICAN BEATS • THE KNUX • KRAAK AND
FIELD • ERIN MCCARLEY • TIFT MERRITT • MGMT • MIDNITE • MIKE FARRIS AND THE ROSELAND RHYTHM REVUE • MOE. • JANELLE MONÁE • MOONALICE • MOTION POTION (SAN
OKKERVIL RIVER • JOHN OLIVER • OUTERNATIONAL • PASSION PIT • PEOPLE UNDER THE STAIRS • PHISH • PHOENIX, THE MAN • PRETTY LIGHTS • THE PROTOMEN
HADOWS FALL • MICHAEL SHOWALTER • TODD SNIDER • SNOOP DOGG • BEN SOLLEE • SONS OF BILL • ST. VINCENT • THE STEELDRIVERS • TANGIERS BLUES BAND • TED LEO
ER ALAN WADE • WAILING SOULS • EVAN WATSON • WHITE RABBITS • WILLIAM ELLIOT WHITMORE • WILCO • LUCINDA WILLIAMS • YEAH YEAH YEAHS • YEASAYER • ZAC BROWN
GROUP • BARONESS • BASSNECTAR • JESSIE BAYLIN • JEFF BECK • DOUG BENSON • BIG SAM'S FUNKY NATION • DIANE BIRCH • THE BLACK KEYS • BLITZEN TRAPPER • BLUES
ATE DROPS • MARGARET CHO • CIRCA SURVIVE • JIMMY CLIFF • CLUTCH • THE CONSTELLATIONS • ELIZABETH COOK • SAMANTHA CRAIN • CROSS CANADIAN RAGWEED • THE
WES • THE DEAD WEATHER • DEADMAU5 • THE DEVIL MAKES THREE • KEVIN DEVINE • DIESELBOY • JARED DIETCH • THE DISCO BISCUITS • DJ EQUAL • DJ LOGIC • THE DODOS
• THE FLAMING LIPS PERFORMING DARK SIDE OF THE MOON, FEATURING STARDEATH AND WHITE DWARFS • JOHN FOGERTY • FRONTIER RUCKUS • GALACTIC • THE GASLIGHT
MES • JAPANDROIDS • SARAH JAROSZ • JAY-Z • JEFFREY ROSS ROASTS BONNAROO • JOHN BUTLER TRIO • JAMEY JOHNSON • JONATHAN SEXTON AND THE BIG LOVE CHAIR
SYSTEM • LES CLAYPOOL • LISSIE • LOCAL NATIVES • LOS AMIGOS INVISIBLES • LOTUS • LUCERO • BAABA MAAL • TIMO MAAS • MANCHESTER ORCHESTRA • IMELDA MAY
ID MICHAELSON • THE MIDDLE EAST • MIGHTY CLOUDS OF JOY • MIIKE SNOW • MONTE MONTGOMERY • THE MOONDOGGIES • MORNING TELEPORTATION • MOTION POTION (SAN
SSIBLE • JULIA NUNES • CONAN O'BRIEN • OK GO • ORGONE • OZOMATLI • PAPER TONGUES • CHELSEA PERETTI • PHOENIX • MIKE POSNER • THE POSTELLES • JOHN PRINE
RUTH AND SALVAGE CO. • FRANK TURNER • UMPHREY'S MCGEE • BARON VAUGHN • WALE • WARPAINT • WEEN • WEEZER • STEVIE WONDER • THE XX • THE YOUNG VEINS • ZAC
ON STATION FEATURING JERRY DOUGLAS • GREGG ALLMAN • THE APACHE RELAY • ARCADE FIRE • ATMOSPHERE • AUNT MARTHA • ANTHONY B • BILL BAILEY • CRAIG BALDO
ELANGER • BEST COAST • BIG BOI • THE BLACK ANGELS • BLACK BOX REVELATION • THE BLACK KEYS • BLACK UHURU • CRISTINA BLACK • LEWIS BLACK • BOOTSY COLLINS
• HANNIBAL BURESS • HAYES CARLL • CHANCELLOR WARHOL • CHEER UP CHARLIE DANIELS • CHIDDY BANG • CHRIS HARFORD AND THE BAND OF CHANGES • CIVIL TWILIGHT
E DAVID MAYFIELD PARADE • DEAS VAIL • THE DECEMBERISTS • DEER TICK • DEERHUNTER • THE DEL MCCOURY BAND AND THE PRESERVATION HALL JAZZ BAND • DEVOTCHKA
TOWNES EARLE • KAREN ELSON • EMINEM • EXPLOSIONS IN THE SKY • FENCES • FINE PEDUNCLE • FLORENCE + THE MACHINE • FORRO IN THE DARK • FREELANCE WHALES
• GOGOL BORDELLO • GRACE POTTER AND THE NOCTURNALS • GRAVEYARD • GREENSKY BLUEGRASS • THE GREGORY BROTHERS • GYPSYPHONIC DISKO • KEVIN HAMMOND
JACKSON • JAMIE MCLEAN BAND • JEFF THE BROTHERHOOD • JOVANOTTI • JUNIP • WIZ KHALIFA • HANNI EL KHATIB • THE KNUX • KOPECKY FAMILY BAND • KYLESA • RAY
• MY MORNING JACKET • NAOMI SHELTON AND THE GOSPEL QUEENS • NEON TREES • NICOLE ATKINS AND THE BLACK SEA • NOFX • TIG NOTARO • OLD CROW MEDICINE SHOW
H • RATATAT • THE REVEREND PEYTON'S BIG DAMN BAND • RIVER CITY EXTENSION • ROBERT PLANT AND BAND OF JOY • ROBYN • HENRY ROLLINS • ROTARY DOWNS • RYAN
TS SHPONGLETRON EXPERIENCE • SLEIGH BELLS • SMITH WESTERNS • BEN SOLLEE • OMAR SOULEYMAN • MAVIS STAPLES • THE STRING CHEESE INCIDENT • THE STROKES
THE WALKMEN • WARREN HAYNES BAND • ABIGAIL WASHBURN • JOHN WATERS • WAVVES • THE WHITE BUFFALO • WIDESPREAD PANIC • AARON "WOODY" WOOD

BONNAROO

WHAT, WHICH, THIS, THAT, THE OTHER

YOU HAVE ARRIVED

For one weekend every June, folks travel from far and wide to a place unlike any other in this country . . .

Held on prime Tennessee farmland, called Great Stage Park, Bonnaroo is where strangers smile and say hello, where hippies hang out with indie rockers, where dancing is as common as standing, where lifelong friendships are forged, and where indelible memories are made.

Since the first Bonnaroo, in 2002, our hope has been to create a diverse community of music fans who not only live together for four days but also ideally grow together through transcendent musical experiences. What began as an idea among a handful of people has blossomed into something beyond our wildest dreams (and we had pretty big dreams!). Every year we try to surprise those who come—many of whom return annually—with both our lineup choices and the festival grounds. Improvisation and collaboration are hallmarks of the Bonnaroo experience.

Our goal has always been to create the very best music and arts festival we can imagine. Another objective has been to create an event that's fresh, exciting, and focused on the extraordinary sense of community that takes place when people come together to share their love of music and culture. A very special spirit is shared by the fans, the artists, the staff, and those local residents who welcome us to Coffee County and Manchester, Tennessee. Nurturing that community spirit and shared experience is our guiding principle as we plan Bonnaroo each year.

And now we bring you *Bonnaroo: What, Which, This, That, The Other*—a celebration of the thousands of musicians who've delivered amazing sets on our stages and who remind us why we make the trek; the countless employees and volunteers who go above and beyond to make sure everyone is safe and having a good time; and last but not least, the melting pot of fans who come together to create the sixth-largest city in Tennessee for a few days each year. We've been blessed to have such talented photographers as Danny Clinch, C. Taylor Crothers, Morgan Harris, Taylor Hill, Jeff Kravitz, Michael Loccisano, Adam Macchia, Doug Mason, Ryan Mastro, and Jason Merritt documenting the many facets of the Bonnaroo experience; their work fills these pages with visceral excitement. In addition to the spectacular photography, we hear from the artists who collaborate, the fans who drink in the music, and our wonderful staffers who help pull it together. They are all here to testify about what Bonnaroo means to them.

As you thumb through these pages, you will take a virtual tour of the Bonnaroo experience—from entering through the arch to cooling off under the Centeroo Fountain, from seeing shows on our stages (What, Which, This, That, and the Other) to hanging out at the Comedy Theater and chilling in the cinema tent. You can hear upcoming bands at the Café stages and find out how you can make a difference while spending time at Planet Roo. Then, when you eventually wander back to your tent, you might catch a few minutes of sleep—or join in a jam with your neighbors. All in all, it becomes pretty clear that we're one big happy family. Enjoy the ride—and we hope to see you soon down on the farm.

—Superfly Presents and AC Entertainment, September 2011

"Bonnaroo 2008 was my first 'Roo. And everybody's first 'Roo is a learning experience. I rolled through the entrance in my busted old truck, loaded to capacity, and the long slow roll to get to our campsite began. The truck couldn't take the heat. At least ten times, I had to pull over and lose my spot in line to let the truck cool down long enough to drive a little farther. As I finally rolled up to my spot with smoke billowing off my engine, determined to get there, I parked, stepped out of my truck—and every person that had passed me while I was parked on the side of the road began to cheer for me and celebrate me making it to Bonnaroo. None of these people knew me, but at that moment they became my family!"

—Tyler Bandy, fan, Westmoreland, TN

"Those four days of 2010 on the farm were the best four days of my twenty-one-year-old life: the cavalcade of cars and RVs entering those beautiful fields, the general understanding and acceptance among the people. It seemed void of prejudice, and that's what I loved most—the people and their excitement and passion for the festival. My benevolent Bonnaroo...."

—Spencer Waddell, fan, Springfield, MO

"Bonnaroo is more than just a music festival, it's a pop-up city with 80,000 people camping together for four days. This creates a one-of-a-kind immersion experience with a true sense of community and escapism."

—Jonathan Mayers, Superfly Presents

"My wife, Sarah, and I were engaged at Bonnaroo in 2007. After driving from Philadelphia with the ring in my pocket, we arrived and immediately headed to Centeroo. As we approached the security line, I began to realize that I didn't think this all the way through. The security guard asked me to empty my pockets, which I did—except for the ring. I leaned toward him and whispered that it was an engagement ring. Sarah and I were engaged fifteen minutes later on the top of the Ferris wheel. Ryan Shaw was the first artist to play that evening. His song 'I Found a Love' became our wedding song."

—Xave Shannon, fan, Philadelphia, PA

"I remember my first day at Bonnaroo. My two friends and I rushed to set up our campsite and get into Centeroo. I can still recall the butterflies in my stomach and the excitement that was boiling inside me while walking to the concert stages. The energy was incredible. It is honestly like being in a completely different world—a wonderful escape from the worries and burdens of everyday life. The four days at Bonnaroo are my favorite days of the year."

—Carlin Salmon, fan, Wildwood, MO

"When the concept of what ultimately became Bonnaroo was first presented to me, I fell in love with the idea immediately. Bonnaroo is an unparalleled experience—it's been great to watch the growth and evolution of the festival over the last ten years."

—Coran Capshaw, cofounder of Bonnaroo

"Bonnaroo is the closest to the crazy factor that we get in Europe. It's such a good atmosphere. Those kids are out there having a good time. And there's so many great bands that play, it's kind of hard to have a bad time there. We like to watch other bands. Every night around one in the morning, they have that band who will go up there and blow your mind for three hours straight."

—Nathan Followill, Kings of Leon

"One of my favorite memories of Bonnaroo was the very first year it came to my little town of Manchester. My family and I live right by the main highway. As I walked up the street to see all the commotion, I was amazed to see cars for miles. There were people everywhere! There was a group on the side of the road playing Frisbee and they asked my brother and me to play with them. Everyone was so nice. From that day on, I told myself as long as they have this festival, I want to be there. I have gone to Bonnaroo every year since."

—Peggy Long, fan, Manchester, TN

"On Thursday, June 12, 2008, I made my first trek into Centeroo. After passing under the famous Bonnaroo arch, I followed the floods of different people who all had one thing in common: Everyone was smiling. And how could we not? It is contagious."

—Amanda Craig, fan, Wilmington, NC

"Before Bonnaroo, I was a horrible dancer. You could never catch me dancing in public. Ever. I was your run-of-the-mill toe tapper/chiller in the back of the show. When I went to my first Bonnaroo, I took a good look around: people dancing and jamming out everywhere. It looked like complete and serious fun! Did everyone dance like a pro and look graceful? Ummmm.... no. Far from it! But I realized that really didn't matter—people were having fun and dancing to a rhythm they felt with the music. Bonnaroo taught me to let go and become a dancer."

—Kelli Dodd, fan, Galloway, OH

IT'S ALL ONE BIG COLLABORATION

Let's assume that any public gathering, at a certain point, depends on collaboration.

By Alan Light

Put a bunch of people together—whether it's a few dozen or tens of thousands—and there has to be some collective sense of cooperation, or disaster is inevitable. Everyone has to agree on some ground rules, some common interest, some vague sense of limits and intentions, and then there's hope for the group.

At a music festival, though, this concept takes on many additional layers. Think about all the factors at play: the audience, the performers, the organizers, the staff, the host community, the physical space

itself—every one of these elements needs to work together to build a place that fosters safety and creativity, freedom and fun. For ten years, over the course of thousands of performances, for hundreds of thousands of attendees, the Bonnaroo Music and Arts Festival has embodied this principle of collaboration.

Let's start at the top. The most visible and obvious manifestation of collaboration at Bonnaroo happens on the stages. The festival has been the site of numerous incomparable musical peaks, one-of-a-kind moments when two (or more) acts join forces and tear the roof off the sucker.

Consider 2009, when the Beastie Boys brought out "a special guest from Queensbridge" named Nas, who wasn't even playing the festival that year, to rip through a song that wouldn't actually be released until two years later. That might have been enough of a surprise for one year—except that the following night, to close the festival, Phish were joined onstage by their "boyhood hero and still hero" Bruce Springsteen (who had hung out and visited the festival's side stages to check out folks like MGMT, Neko Case, and Band of Horses after his Saturday-night set) for a romp through "Mustang Sally" and two songs from *Born in the U.S.A.* It was a long way from 2006, when the Disco Biscuits and Umphrey's McGee merged their sets into one nonstop mega-jam—or was it?

The Bonnaroo brain trust hails from New Orleans and Tennessee, areas where

musical cross-pollination proliferates, which might explain why this idea of putting artists together and seeing what happens is such an important part of Bonnaroo's mission that a centerpiece of the festival is its annual "SuperJam."

In 2007, that meant a Friday-night set featuring Led Zeppelin's John Paul Jones, the Roots' monster drum master ?uestlove, and Ben Harper raging through a barrage of Zeppelin songs, plus choice selections like "Them Changes" and "Superstition."

The SuperJam appearance was so meaningful to Harper, he later told me, that it helped determine the direction of his next album. As for Jones (who would join Robert Plant and Jimmy Page just a few months later for Led Zep's legendary, one-off London reunion), he spent the weekend wandering the grounds in shorts, with a big grin and a mandolin, delighted to sit in with anyone who asked, including Gillian Welch, who dubbed him "the King of Rock and Bluegrass." He became one of those figures, like Warren Haynes and

Robert Randolph, who seem to pop up onstage every time you turn around.

In 2011, the festival brought it all back home by celebrating New Orleans royalty, as Dr. John, the original Meters, and Allen Toussaint joined forces for the first-ever live performance of the full album that gave the event its name, 1974's *Desitively Bonnaroo*. That funkdafied set wasn't the only one for the man born Mac Rebennack, who had just been inducted into the Rock and Roll Hall of Fame. Dr. John was also the glue for this most recent go-round of the SuperJam, grooving away alongside Dan Auerbach of the Black Keys and drummer Patrick Hallahan of My Morning Jacket.

Most of the musical collaborations at Bonnaroo, though, aren't so high-profile. Rather, they happen on the smaller stages or by the artists' catering tent or even out in the campgrounds, where old friends meet or new friends find each other and have the rare opportunity to play just for the fun of it. The headliners get the attention, but music is everywhere

for those four days in Manchester, Tennessee, and the simple joy of playing together extends from distant campsites to the main stages.

But none of these creative hookups could ever take place without a fundamental sense of cooperation and trust between the eighty thousand (give or take) fans who make the trek to the farm and the folks in charge of the festival. Most notable has been the willingness of everyone involved to allow Bonnaroo's musical identity to evolve over the years.

Though everything from bluegrass (Del McCoury) to gospel (the Blind Boys of Alabama), hip-hop (De La Soul) to soul (James Brown) was in the mix from the festival's earliest days, the anchor artists of the first few 'Roos—Widespread Panic, Trey Anastasio, various offshoots of the Grateful Dead, the String Cheese Incident—were firmly rooted in the jam-band scene.

After a few years, things naturally began to expand. Hip-hop and hard rock moved from the side stages to the top of the bill, and while there were certainly

purists offended by the arrival of Jay-Z and Eminem or Tool and Metallica as Bonnaroo headliners, the vast majority of the audience knew that it shouldn't matter what the music is labeled—everything should be welcome as long as it's made by great live performers. (Tool's face-melting, powerhouse set in 2007, like the brutal beauty of Nine Inch Nails' in 2009, actually proved to be a seamless and unforgettable addition to the Bonnaroo stew.)

This growth has happened, though, only because the audience has had faith in those making the decisions. Over the years, after experiencing the festival and its ever-transforming vision, plenty of people return for the ride. It's why thousands of tickets are sold every year before any artists are even announced: Folks know they want to be there for the total immersion—and the immersion is most definitely complete; once you're on those campgrounds, there's nowhere else to go until it's time to leave.

The Bonnaroo team is well aware that the musicians and the audience aren't the only parts of the festival community they need to involve and respect. Collaboration at the event also extends to the local population in Coffee County (home to approximately fifty thousand Middle Tennesseans, and maybe best known as being located close to the George Dickel whiskey distillery), where Bonnaroo has now become one of the crucial elements of the economy. After the initial skepticism—and who wouldn't be concerned, hearing that tens of thousands of hippies and freaks would be descending on the small town of Manchester?—the locals have seen that

the festival is a boon to their area, leading to jobs and construction (according to one study, adding fourteen million dollars to business revenues) and contributing more than a million dollars to local schools and civic efforts.

Then there's the festival staff itself, the hundreds of people working security and cleaning up and directing traffic, all maintaining the proper tone of liberty and discipline. Many of these workers are brought up from New Orleans each year (employment that has been particularly welcome in the aftermath of Hurricane Katrina), and some have become so familiar that they are practically celebrities themselves.

Without getting too metaphysical, perhaps the ultimate partnership happens between the festival and the seven hundred acres of land on which this glorious mayhem occurs. The Bonnaroo team has made a year-round commitment to sustainability on the site, and has been honored for its environmental efforts. By 2011, more than half of all the festival's waste was diverted from landfills, thanks to recycling and composting, and nine hundred metric tons of CO_2 were offset. Efforts are continually being made to reduce the festival's carbon footprint and to increase the recycling and composting on-site. The culmination of the environmental mission statement is Planet Roo, a village that is dedicated to promoting an environmentally and socially responsible lifestyle and that features a solar-powered performance stage.

In 2007, Bonnaroo strengthened its commitment to Manchester by acquiring Great Stage Park—more than five hundred

acres of the festival site. As permanent roads and structures are added, built not only for 'Roos of the future but also for other events throughout the year, the alliance between this team and its hosts only becomes more solidified.

Of course, Bonnaroo's greatest collaboration is unquestionably the peaceful coexistence of the fans, year after year. The most amazing improvisations happen not on the stages but in the campgrounds, where an entire city is constructed for a weekend and people from all over the world join as one nation under a groove, choosing to surrender conventional luxuries, to often battle the elements, and to help each other have a great time. The simple act of playing a song together seems pretty insignificant next to the creation of a harmonious village dedicated to sharing and enjoying an experience unlike any other.

College kids having the adventure of their young lives. Corporate executives playing hooky from their pressure-packed urban existences. Old friends now living in different cities organizing their schedules around an annual rendezvous in Manchester (I certainly know some of these, and I bet you do too). Side by side, in blazing heat or drenching rain, from early morning to impossibly late at night, they live and eat and dance and laugh together, and combine to form something so much larger than themselves.

When all the elements align, it can make for one of those magical, unforgettable Bonnaroo moments. Radiohead's epic appearance, the White Stripes howling through a dusty sunset, Stevie Wonder leading a joyous sing-along, My Morning Jacket testifying into a deluge at three A.M., Merle Haggard, Manu Chao, Wanda Jackson, Regina Spektor, Girl Talk . . . well, you can choose your own favorites. In ways immense and tiny, long-term and sudden, collaboration is what Bonnaroo is all about, and what makes it the greatest weekend-long, twenty-four-hour-a-day, seven-hundred-acre, eighty-thousand-person jam session on Earth.

"Humankind is the greatest expression of the universe, and Bonnaroo is the greatest expression of humankind."

—Ryan Bowering, fan, Shoreline, WA

"Bonnaroo provides a platform to expose our community to so many different ways of thought and causes that are helping to make our world a better place for everyone. We've always believed that opening yourself up to new experiences, people, and ideas builds compassion and a sense of community, and we take our responsibility to do so very seriously. While everyone is having such a great time, it's also an amazing place to learn and contribute to creating a better world. Planet Roo is really the epicenter of this learning. It features nonprofits that work on issues such as poverty, environmentalism, social justice, and water conservation. With so much turmoil in our world, and misleading information conveyed in sound bites through mainstream media, we provide an alternate outlet for learning. We hope to make positive activism a natural part of this generation.

Environmentalism has always been a major focus for us—just trying to do the best we can to mitigate any negative impact we may have on the world. Global warming being such a profound issue is not lost on us. We have a great team that creates the event and really seeks to devise optimal solutions to building this temporary city, and there is a process of constant evaluation in place. From our department heads to our audience, everyone is contributing ideas about how we can do things better. There is a sense of pride in having won the International Greener Festival award every year, and now there is an obligation to help others learn how they can reduce their impact as well."

—Rich Goodstone, Superfly Presents

"We played with Kirk Hammett from Metallica one year; if the 'eighth-grade me' could see what was happening, he would be losing his mind. There have been moments at Bonnaroo where you are having an out-of-body experience—to be playing and see Kirk Hammett onstage with you. It's such a surreal feeling."

—Jim James, My Morning Jacket

My Morning Jacket and Kirk Hammett
(third from right), June 13, 2008

"I'm very pleased that the whole concept of 'festival' is still viable.

It's probably the best way to really enjoy music, because you can go there and spend a weekend and you're not worried about going to work or getting home. You can camp out and relax and have a good time and immerse yourself in the music. That was the spirit we always tried to evoke at Grateful Dead shows.

Bonnaroo is probably as much fun as you can have in one place, and the thing that impresses me most about it is that the festival has grown to encompass more than just jam bands. When you go there, you can pretty much hear the whole spread of music that's being made today, and that's very exciting. There's no one genre of music that's more important than others.

When I go to Bonnaroo, I like to stay until the very last moment and see as many acts as I can. My wife and I went on the Ferris wheel the last time we were there. We saw Jackie Greene; we saw Bill Frisell. Just wandering around, we saw all kinds of acts. I saw My Morning Jacket and I remember enjoying them a whole lot.

Just the idea of being able to wander around and follow your ears to hear some music that you haven't happened to hear before is a great thing. I like to see roots music. I like to see improvisational music. I even like electronica and dance music. The Grateful Dead was all of those influences fused together. I think it's important that everybody understands that there's so much variety and richness and range in music that you're doing yourself a disservice if you only listen to the blues, if you only listen to pop music, if you only listen to rap. There's just so much, and it all hangs together in that it's American music."

—Phil Lesh

ABOVE: Bill Kreutzmann and Mickey Hart, June 12, 2004
BELOW: Phil Lesh and Bob Weir, June 23, 2002

"I wound up walking around Bonnaroo for twelve straight hours, till six in the morning. I had a really good time. I started out at midnight at the Meters, and Warren [Haynes] was sitting in with them. Then we wandered over to Sound Tribe Sector 9. I had never seen them before, but I was really into it. It's a kind of house music flavor, but with some other jam-band-influence stuff going on. I started to walk away before the encore, and I just thought, 'Shit, I'll just walk back and maybe I could play.' So I ran all the way back by the stage, and I'd never met them or heard them before until just then. I was thinking, 'Well, this is a whole different mode of improvising than I'm used to.' In this case, the bass lines are supposed to be more repetitive, which I like. I have to tweak my brain—all this self-consciousness thinking, 'I'm supposed to do that. I'm not supposed to do this.' That's what has to go away—all that thinking—until you're just standing there and letting it happen."

—Mike Gordon, Phish

"On November 1, 1978, I went with my sister Kristy to see Bruce Springsteen at Jadwin Gym in Princeton, New Jersey. He opened the show with 'Badlands,' played 'Darkness on the Edge of Town,' 'Prove It All Night,' 'Thunder Road,' 'Jungleland,' 'Backstreets'—it was just mind-blowing. . . . He then encored with 'Rosalita,' 'Born to Run,' and, I think, maybe even a third song. I had just turned fourteen one month earlier. Kristy was sixteen. It made me want to be a musician.

My sister lost a long battle with cancer only weeks before Bonnaroo in 2009, and while she couldn't be there in body, she was there in spirit. Bruce was kind enough to play my request, 'Bobby Jean,' and I thought of Kristy while we played.

I tell this story because it expresses a feeling that I know many people share: that Bruce is so much more than an entertainer. His music is an integral part of the fabric of my life. He has a huge heart that pours out of every note he plays and sings, in every song, at every concert. This is the elusive quality of the master musician. He cares."

—Trey Anastasio

ABOVE: Galactic's Stanton Moore and Mike Gordon of Phish during the SuperJam, June 14, 2003
BELOW: Trey Anastasio and Bruce Springsteen when Springsteen joined Phish onstage, June 14, 2009

"The cooperation and support we get from the local community is essential to the success of Bonnaroo. We've had a long and productive relationship with city and county officials and so many citizens of Coffee County. Without their help, we wouldn't be here today."

—Ashley Capps, AC Entertainment

"I've been coming to Bonnaroo for three years now. I wouldn't have come back after the first time if it wasn't for all the great amenities and services that are provided for people with disabilities by Bonnaroo's awesome access coordinator, Laura Grunfeld, and her team. The access program is just great. There are platforms everywhere so that wheelchair users can see the stage, and there are sign-language interpreters. There is a great accessible camping situation. I have been to several other music festivals, mostly in California, and a lot of them have some services for disabled people, but there are gaps that still need to be filled. I have never been anywhere else that filled all the gaps as well as Bonnaroo."

—Tyler Rudy, fan, Berkeley, CA

"The Bobbleheads were first created in 2003. I worked with one of my artists, Sara Lee Tarat, to create the cartoon caricatures that were blown up to large scale. We then had a shop in New Orleans—Stronghold Studios—make the heads and bodies out of Styrofoam and papier-mâché and paint and sealer. We make them over every year using a different theme—although they will always be mullet Bobbleheads."

—Russ Bennett, head of visual design, Bonnaroo

"Bonnaroo became a partner with us from the very first show they put on. From the beginning, they were organized."

—David Pennington, mayor of Coffee County, TN

"Bonnaroo has always tried to be good to our community, and I think that's made a big difference to people. For the city, they paid $10,000 a year for three years to help build a skateboard park, and they bought new band uniforms for the high school. One of our senior citizen centers was about to close, but Bonnaroo gave us $12,000 to keep it open."

—Betty Superstein, mayor of Manchester, TN

WHAT

"Certainly, one of the initial inspirations for Bonnaroo—along with Jazz Fest in New Orleans and some big European festivals—was Phish's major festivals. As fans of the band, we saw what they did—how they treated their fans, incorporated art installations, and how they fostered community at these events—which served as a model for what we were looking to do. Many of our key staff, even to this day, came from their team. That connection has always made performances by the band members—especially when Phish played in 2009—extra-special."

—Rick Farman, Superfly Presents

Phish, June 12, 2009

"I was beyond excited to see Pearl Jam, and so were the eighty thousand other people packed in tightly. We danced, jammed, and partied with all the people around us. Then the first, unmistakable chords of 'Better Man' began. Eddie Vedder's softened voice sang the first part while the crowd's voice lingered underneath. The chorus came along and Eddie paused and let the crowd take over. At that moment, being fairly close to the front, I looked back and saw an ocean of people behind us singing the words, and it hit me: There are thousands of people here, of different races, gender, religion, political views—hell, even differences on food preferences—but at this one moment we all agree on one thing: that this song is fucking awesome. In a world where people are separated by so many things, music brought eighty thousand people together. I was so blessed to be a part of it. For the first time, I truly felt the power of music."

—Hannah Williams, fan, Statesville, NC

Pearl Jam, June 14, 2008

"Wait till I tell Mom
Stevie Wonder
stayed for my set."

—Jay-Z

PREVIOUS PAGES: Arcade Fire,
June 10, 2011

Jay-Z, June 12, 2010

"We did this festival called Bonnaroo. We did 2.5 hours. And there's eighty thousand people. It was just amazing. We played loads of new stuff. We did whole sections of quiet piano songs, and it sounds like the most grotesque self-indulgent nonsense, but it probably is my favorite gig for years and years and years."

—Thom Yorke, Radiohead

Thom Yorke with Radiohead, June 18, 2006

"I'm going to be your teacher. Don't mess up my words."

—Stevie Wonder

"I don't think I have ever felt more joy surge through my body than when I sang along with Stevie Wonder. He cried out the opening 'Ay-ay-ay-ays' of 'Master Blaster (Jammin')' and we repeated them back to him. He then deemed the crowd as 'Stevie Wonder's Chorus of Voices.' I love it when I have a chance to tell people I was in Stevie Wonder's Chorus of Voices!"

—Mandy Zlotek, fan, St. Johns, MI

Stevie Wonder, June 12, 2010

"This is my first Bonnaroo [2004], but I knew about it because I had friends that were involved. It's the first festival in America in a really long time to be successful, if for no other reason than celebrating music. People come and hang out in the middle of nowhere to smell each other's funk and listen to great, eclectic music from all corners of the industry. To get this many people together in one place, and be peaceful, that's the power of this weekend."

—Dave Matthews

Dave Matthews Band, June 13, 2010

"The really great thing about Bonnaroo is
that you get to hang out with old friends."

—Dave Schools, Widespread Panic

Widespread Panic, June 12, 2011

"Whether it's the artists or the promoters or people who are dishing out food or water, Bonnaroo is a big community thing, and fans can sense that. They can feel when it's a positive thing. The bands want to be a part of something that's good, that's fun, and that's exciting. It's like the Woodstock of the Southeast. I could tell from the beginning it was something big when we saw all those folks coming out for the very first time. It was truly a unique and special moment."

—Sunny Ortiz, Widespread Panic

"We're proud to represent the state of Tennessee. We're the locals, so it's good to get it out there that the South can put on a good festival."

—Nathan Followill, Kings of Leon

"There are very, very few times when I've felt really proud of what we've accomplished. This is one of those times."

—Caleb Followill, Kings of Leon

ABOVE: Kings of Leon, June 12, 2004
BELOW: Kings of Leon, June 11, 2010

"Bonnaroo, for me, was an experience of extremes. The weather, when I attended in 2004, came in two flavors: rains that I would call a monsoon and temperatures so hot that I felt like I was standing in front of an industrial-size furnace, at full blast, with the doors open. I don't remember any middle ground. I would sit in my parked car and turn on the air-conditioning just to cool off.

But rather than slow me down, the extreme weather was inspiring, just like Steve Winwood belting out a version of 'Back in the High Life' from the main stage that called the hair on the back of my neck to attention, or Beth Orton sweetly crooning, quite fittingly in fact, Bob Dylan's 'Buckets of Rain,' from one of the smaller stages. The String Cheese Incident covered the Red Hot Chili Peppers. Les Claypool dazzled. Trey Anastasio, well, he blew my mind.

Bonnaroo wasn't simply a music festival. For me, it was a once-in-a-lifetime road trip from New York to Tennessee that began after Wilco played the Chance in Poughkeepsie, New York, on a Monday night, and ended when Wilco played the main stage at Bonnaroo that following Friday afternoon. Bonnaroo was not just an event, it was an experience. Bonnaroo gave me and the tens of thousands of other folks in attendance that weekend in 2004 a chance to stake a claim, to set up shop, pitch a tent, circle the wagons, and build a community. After years and years of following our favorite bands around the country, sleeping in cars, eating at highway rest stops, exploring America, and becoming Woody Guthrie or Bob Dylan for a few days, everyone had come home to Bonnaroo."

—John W. Barry, music writer,
Poughkeepsie Journal

PREVIOUS PAGES (clockwise from top left): Eminem, June 11, 2011; Damian Marley and Nas, June 11, 2010; Beastie Boys, June 12, 2009; Snoop Dogg, June 14, 2009

Jeff Tweedy of Wilco, June 17, 2007

"Sixty percent of the audience couldn't name the four Roots albums. I'm more interested in doing a music revue—being a teacher and going through an entire spectrum of music, some ours, some not ours."

—?uestlove, the Roots

PREVIOUS PAGES: B. B. King,
June 14, 2008

LEFT: ?uestlove of the Roots,
June 15, 2007

NEXT PAGES: Jack Johnson, June 14,
2008; Ben Harper, June 16, 2007

"My perception is that at Bonnaroo, all the corporate elements are left at the door—or at least the freeway, or wherever they're left. It's about a love of music. It starts and ends with that. To have Metallica there seems so obvious. We've always felt that Metallica exists in its own bubble. We've never really felt a part of a scene or a movement. We've always considered ourselves a little awkward—kind of the underdog, the loners. So we've always been pretty comfortable going into different environments, because we never felt that we really represented anything in particular.

We go all over and play festivals in Europe almost every year, but the great festival season in Europe never really happened here. In America, it's either a hard-rock thing, or an alternative thing, or a jam thing. But there are festivals in Europe where it's not about a specific thing; it's about all of it. It's a whole musical landscape, and it's about variety. It seems that there's finally something happening in America the last couple years, with Bonnaroo being the leader of the pack."

—Lars Ulrich, Metallica

"Young people are starting to use festivals as a way of balancing out what has been an isolated generation—between computers and video games and that sort of thing. Instead of hanging out in the park, like we used to do, or hanging out at the mall, like the previous generation, kids today go home, go in their room, turn their computer on, or text on their cell phone. It's a very isolated way of socializing. Now, all of a sudden that's being balanced out by festivals, where they are coming out and being with other young people. It's a very healthy thing to balance new technology with festivals."

—Steven Van Zandt, Bruce Springsteen and the E Street Band

ABOVE: Lars Ulrich of Metallica,
June 13, 2008
BELOW: Bruce Springsteen and
Steven Van Zandt, June 13, 2009

NEXT PAGES: Bruce Springsteen,
June 13, 2009

BELOW: Al Green, June 12, 2009
RIGHT: James Brown, June 15, 2003

"I want to come down there and dance
  with you."

—Al Green

"For people who work a normal nine-to-five job, it's really a chance to come lead an alternate life. You come out with your tent, and you stay somewhere else for four days, and run around in the mud and the rain, and eat and drink, and just have a good time and meet a lot of new people. You can walk around this huge magical place where you can see almost any type of music that you could ever dream of seeing. People are always looking for an escape from reality and their normal lives, and that's one reason why so many people love Bonnaroo, because you can come out and be a different person, forget about who you are and what you'd normally do.

We always get excited about Bonnaroo because you get to reach so many people at once. Every type of music is represented. The jam-friendly community is definitely one part of it, but every year it's gotten more and more varied. It's still one of the best places to bring people together, from all walks of life. It's unpredictable. Something new and special happens every year. There is something about the setup—something comfortable and familiar—that makes me feel like it belongs to everyone. [It's] like the planners thought about comfort and realism. Plus, I've gotten to see several of my heroes perform there and have been inspired countless times by people I had heard were good but had never gotten the chance to check out.

We always try and stay for the whole thing, because playing is fun, but that's just one part of it. We love hanging out and going to see all the bands. Lots of our friends are there from other bands and from home, because it's kind of close to Kentucky. It's nice for us to just come and relax and take the four days off and have a good time."

—Jim James, My Morning Jacket

"There's a certain feeling of togetherness at Bonnaroo. The crowd is very attentive. Bonnaroo crowds cheer when it's time to cheer and go crazy when it's time to go crazy and be quiet when it's time to be quiet. It's inundated with music fans, so when we have new material, it provides a platform for us to come out and either try new stuff or play the whole album from start to finish. Bonnaroo is probably the only festival that will let us play for three hours straight."

—Patrick Hallahan, My Morning Jacket

My Morning Jacket, June 10, 2011

"Seeing Neil Young and Crazy Horse at Bonnaroo was one of my favorite musical moments of my life."

—Ben Harper

Neil Young and Crazy Horse,
June 13, 2003

"Bonnaroo is a very different kind of gig. All of the others, it's the Police show. We've been rehearsing for four months. The band is so tight you could open a bottle with it. At Bonnaroo, the mission there—at least, my mission anyway—is to completely deconstruct the whole thing. I've almost got Sting and Andy convinced we're going to go onstage at Bonnaroo and we're going to play five songs for half an hour each. And we're going to tear it all down and rip it up."

—Stewart Copeland, the Police

"I went to management and said, 'I don't care if we do this for free, we gotta be there. This is just too cool a thing. There are too many young kids who may know who we are, but don't really know who we are. We need to be there in front of those kids.' You get all the good bands together, all the fans camping out for days. If you're lucky, it rains like hell and everybody can get good and wet and muddy. And a lot of great music is played, and everybody has a lot of fun. It's the same thing [as at Woodstock]. It's the next generation."

—Butch Trucks, the Allman Brothers Band

ABOVE: The Police, June 16, 2007
BELOW: The Allman Brothers Band,
June 10, 2005

"Robert Plant and Metallica and
B.B. King and the Allman Brothers—
that's an eclectic group of bands.
It's a real fun thing to be part of."

—Mike McCready, Pearl Jam

"I felt really at home. I'm a sweaty
hippie myself."

—Wiz Khalifa

FIRST ROW: Wiz Khalifa, June 11, 2011; Ben Harper, June 13, 2003; Trey Anastasio, June 23, 2002; the Dead Weather, June 12, 2010; Erykah Badu, June 14, 2009
SECOND ROW: Wild Magnolias, June 16, 2007; Tenacious D, June 11, 2010; Beck, June 17, 2006; Jay-Z, June 12, 2010; Alison Krauss, June 10, 2005
THIRD ROW: Jimmy Cliff, June 12, 2010; Damian Marley, June 11, 2010; John Fogerty, June 13, 2010; Emmylou Harris, June 14, 2003; Oysterhead, June 16, 2006
FOURTH ROW: Erykah Badu and Snoop Dogg, June 14, 2009; Sting, June 16, 2007; Tom Petty, June 16, 2006; Dave Matthews and Trey Anastasio, June 11, 2004

NEXT PAGES: Bob Dylan, June 11, 2004

WHICH

"Any festival where you can see My Morning Jacket and Lil Wayne is OK by me."

—Win Butler, Arcade Fire

PREVIOUS PAGES: The Flaming Lips, June 11, 2010

Lil Wayne, June 10, 2011

"What's so great about Bonnaroo is that people can get into the spirit and play along. Because things might happen: It might rain, it might be muddy, it might be cold. But if people have the right attitude and the right spirit, you can still have the time of your life. So my mission is to say, 'Let's make sure this is everybody's perfect night.'

I'm adaptable to the point where, if it's bad, we're going to make it good, but if it's good, we're going to add to it. I know how powerful an experience it can be. So for those that see the Flaming Lips at Bonnaroo, I'm hoping it's a life-changing experience. But it isn't seeing the bands that's the great thing; it's this moment in your life when you're there with your friends and it's just a powerful time.

The atmosphere is always better at Bonnaroo because people aren't there to see a whole range of your songs. In a way, they get a short, explosive set that's stuck in between all these other bands. It really is just another experience in their long day of doing stuff. In a way, it almost works better, because we come out and play a forty-five-minute set, and it's like nothing you've seen. Hopefully, there'll be something after us that's great and something before us that's great, because it's the overall experience that people are there for. Some bands take themselves too serious. They think, 'Oh everybody's gonna be watching us.' I tell them, 'They're not really watching you. They're . . . thinking about having sex tonight. Don't worry about it. You're just there filling in the time to give them some stuff to talk about.' And that's my job. I'll give everybody something to talk about at three o'clock in the morning. When they go back to their tents, they'll talk about the Flaming Lips throwing balloons and having animals and confetti and these crazy films.

If I wasn't playing at Bonnaroo, I'd still want to be here. It's an adventure. We've got to live it with intensity, and it is easy to get inspired here."

—Wayne Coyne, the Flaming Lips

The Flaming Lips, June 11, 2010

"When an audience is outdoors, you need to grab them a little bit harder and get them involved and, at least at some point, make the whole set run a little faster and be more accessible than you would in a theater."

—David Byrne

David Byrne, June 12, 2009

NEXT PAGES (clockwise from top left): The Gaslight Anthem, June 11, 2010; Willie Nelson, June 13, 2008; Primus, June 10, 2011; Weezer, June 12, 2010

Thomas Mars of Phoenix, June 13, 2010

PREVIOUS PAGES: Cedric Bixler-Zavala of
the Mars Volta, June 13, 2009; Karen O of
the Yeah Yeah Yeahs, June 12, 2009; Trent
Reznor, June 13, 2009

"The first time we played Bonnaroo [in 2009], we thought the excited frenzy that happened before we took the stage wasn't for us. Our album [*Wolfgang Amadeus Phoenix*] had just come out, and we didn't know it was going to be successful. We played a not-so-musical performance because the crowd was so loud and it was so exciting just to look at people getting on top of each other. The second time [in 2010] we were very nervous because everybody kept on talking about our first time. We didn't want it to be some sort of victory lap. I remember the performance being tighter and more violent than the year before. What I like about Bonnaroo is how wild it is. From our experience, extreme conditions are always better for a live show."

—Thomas Mars, Phoenix

"What is it, the next Woodstock?"

—Bill Nershi, the String Cheese Incident

ABOVE: The String Cheese Incident,
June 15, 2007

RIGHT: Wolfmother, June 17, 2007

"I played a lot of festivals over the last twelve years, so most of the time I'm jaded about them. [In 2006] I went to a yoga camp, and then I got off the plane and the next day I went to play and sing at a thing called Bonnaroo. For all I knew, it was a coffeehouse. I had no idea. And when we walked out onstage, there's like sixty thousand people. And not only that: They were really in tune with the music, and I thought, 'Well, there's some hope out there.' Because I think that people [at Bonnaroo] are connected in the music world by different strings than they used to be. [Other festivals] advertise on radio and get a bunch of corporate bands out in the place and take people's money in the middle of a field somewhere and send them home. That's what [previous] festivals were, and this was not like that. This was really, really impressive and really, really musical. I became sort of a born-again festival player after that. I was so relaxed about it, not really knowing what it was. I just came out and approached it the same way as if we were playing a theater or a small club or anything. It wasn't really different. But you can't help but feel a rush of energy of sixty thousand people, as opposed to six thousand people. It's nice to look out and see people and feel people that get it. The fact that you can get that many people in one place who are not getting into fistfights—it's pretty cool. They aren't dumb-asses.

I'm a little bit of a geek about sound, and I'm not thrilled about outdoor sound, but I think that Bonnaroo transcends that. It creates a certain amount of static noise that's sort of spiritual, if you will. I found it easier to play ballads for those sixty thousand kids than I have sometimes playing for just thousands."

—Ben Folds

Ben Folds, June 16, 2006

"I've been kicking around at Bonnaroo for years, and I know this festival ground really well. A lot of good memories are married to this place: SuperJams with Les Claypool, jamming with Kirk Hammett, a tribute to Tom Waits, our own sets, and good hangouts. Everything makes it, for us, a central festival in the States. I was excited that they were very forward-thinking to expand the international lineup. In general, it's a very family spirit because musicians that have a certain intensity of feeling resonate with each other. There's a lot of energy there. As different as styles might be, energy is the thread, because live music is essentially about energy. It's most important to bring [international music] to an American festival because the rest of the world is already schooled in listening to each other. We all grew up listening to music that was English-speaking, for the most part, or French- and Italian- and Arabic-speaking. We listen to all of it without having that supposed barrier that Americans always say: 'We don't understand anything.' What don't you understand? You don't listen to music with your mind. Your subconscious listens to music; your heart listens to music. I have a lot of experience listening to music that I supposedly don't understand. It's actually a more pure form of information. Jimi Hendrix and Chuck Berry and Creedence and the Sex Pistols and Fugazi and Henry Rollins and Johnny Cash and the Clash—they translated perfectly to most of the countries of the world without anybody knowing the actual lyrical meaning. It's an emotional message that really says it all. So in America, it's particularly important to do that because people seem to have the language barrier. But it's an illusion; it's not real. This music is there as the purest form of communication. There's no reason to rob yourself of that music. It's really just like stealing from yourself—not listening to music in other languages."

—Eugene Hütz, Gogol Bordello

Eugene Hütz of Gogol Bordello,
June 14, 2008

"There's not a lot of angst. I'm probably spreading the most angst out of anybody here. I just haven't seen enough nudity here at Bonnaroo."

—Les Claypool

Les Claypool, June 13, 2008

"Bonnaroo '04 was one of the best concerts we've ever had. It started off really, really oppressingly hot, and then all of a sudden it just magically got a little cooler. The stage got darker, and the audience started to kind of razz up a little more, and then the drops of water started falling, and everybody started to get a little more excited and more excited. Then the rain just started pouring down, and instead of getting sad or depressed, everybody was ready to be cooled off. The sky looked so weird, and the whole thing was so surreal anyway—to play in front of that many people, and to be able to share getting wet and not getting electrocuted and a near-death experience. It's hard to put into words how magical it was for all. And when we got done, we felt like we'd just won the Super Bowl or something."

—Jim James, My Morning Jacket

"It was one of the most electrifying experiences of my life personally and within the band's existence. It was just something out of the heavens, that's for sure. I don't think I've ever in my entire life been more pumped up and more nervous and anxious to hit a stage. We had to pay off the weatherman, but he came through for us and brought that thunderstorm right on through."

—Patrick Hallahan, My Morning Jacket

Jim James of My Morning Jacket,
June 12, 2004

"We played 'Bobbaroo' the first time in '03. We were about to release *Decoration Day*. It was our very first time to go out in a bus. We had a short bus, about three-quarter scale, with no back lounge. We were sure the other buses were laughing at our little bus, but we were out of our van for the first time in nearly a thousand shows on the road, so we were excited. We played a really good, sweaty set, and afterward, Brad (our drummer) met Kimberly, who he married a few months later. They have a beautiful daughter, who is three now.

The second time was in '05. We were on year two of the Dirty South Tour, and it was over a hundred degrees. We played a really good set (as I remember it), but that was a bumpy summer for us, and we were somewhat less than healthy.

The third and best time we played was in '08. We had what looked on paper to be a lousy slot (noon, Friday), but it turned out to be incredible. A ton of people came out, and it was unseasonably cool (for Bonnaroo): about eighty-five degrees with a breeze. I bet over forty thousand people saw our set, and we played really well. We loaded out and drove straight to Denver for a festival show out there the next day.

In '09 I played twice. I played on Friday (I think) solo with my side band, the Screwtopians, and played right after the Low Anthem (who I love). Next day we played backing up Booker T. Jones in front of a big, hot, sweaty crowd and had a really good set. Backing up Booker was always a thrill. Afterward I went to see Bruce Springsteen play one of the most amazing sets I've ever seen in my life."

—Patterson Hood, Drive-By Truckers

"On our way to Bonnaroo, we'd been through a right old mess. We were traveling into the festival when the air-con on our tour bus collapsed. All the fellas stripped off their clothes, and we marched on to the 'Roo.... Shortly after, we came across a fire truck stopped in the road. There had been a 'pig fat spillage'! Essentially, a layer of grease had coated the road for miles. We were delayed for a while as the authorities tried to clean it with water, but with little success. We started up again and carried on to the festival, twelve naked dudes, the fumes of cooking pig fat bursting through the windows. We smelt mighty swine as we trotted into town!"

—Olly Peacock, Gomez

ABOVE: Drive-By Truckers with
Booker T. Jones, June 13, 2009
BELOW: Gomez, June 12, 2004

"We played Bonnaroo shortly after *Boxer* came out [in 2007], and it was one of the early indicators that things were going to go well over the next year. People didn't really know the record yet. The tent was packed all the way back, and people were listening and really excited. It was one of the first times in the U.S. that we had a warm, receptive festival audience. We started to feel there was something changing and growing, and it was exhilarating. It really helped us, I think, because there were so many people who went away from that show excited."

—Aaron Dessner, the National

"The festival has always been something of a homecoming for us ever since we kicked off the first set of the festival back in '02. This will be our fifth appearance in Manchester, having also performed at Bonnaroo in '05 and '07, and again in 2010 with the Dave Rawlings Machine, in addition to making guest appearances with John Prine and Mumford and Sons. Some of the best music at Bonnaroo is in the campground: guitars twangin', djembes, dudes with Oregon plates singing 'Wagon Wheel.' Bonnaroo rolls up all the other festivals across the land and lights 'em up."

—Ketch Secor, Old Crow Medicine Show

ABOVE: The National, June 11, 2010
BELOW: Old Crow Medicine Show,
June 11, 2011

"Playing 'No Woman No Cry' with Trey was a moment of things coming full circle for me. It touched me deeply."

—Matisyahu

"In 2002, it was burning hot—and for days, apparently. In the middle of our set, the skies opened up and the audience went crazy. It's as if they thought we were responsible for the rain. They loved us for it! Around the time we were basking in our new status as Bonnaroo gods, the top of our tent filled with water, and it all poured into the onstage monitor board. Smoke started coming out, and it died completely. We kept on playing, eventually realizing we could turn one of the front fill speakers around toward us and then we'd still be able to hear each other and play. An adventure! Luckily Ed's eighteenth-century bass did not get wet."

—Béla Fleck

ABOVE: Matisyahu, June 18, 2006
BELOW: Béla Fleck (second from right)
and the Flecktones, June 18, 2006

"The crowd that travels to Bonnaroo are the most open people you're going to play to. They come to hear familiar stuff but also to discover new artists, and they embrace both with the same attention and love."

—Ray LaMontagne

"There's always the potential, when you put eighty thousand people in one spot, that politics are going to come up. I look at the lineup and think that there is a zeitgeist quality to a lot of the bands and performers, and hopefully it will be a good moment of community and discourse."

—Nick Harmer, Death Cab for Cutie

"I went to Bonnaroo 2008 after retiring from my career. Growing up in the '60s and '70s, my taste in music was still the great bands of that time. Bonnaroo turned me on to a lot of new music and renewed my interest in a lifestyle that had slipped away. My love for live music was restored, and I now go to as many shows as I'm able."

—Bart Robinson, fan, Bloomsburg, PA

"If Woodstock had been like this, we would have never left!"

—Stephen Stills

FIRST ROW: Sharon Jones and the Dap-Kings, June 14, 2008; Buddy Guy, June 17, 2006; Ben Gibbard of Death Cab for Cutie, June 15, 2008; Regina Spektor, June 13, 2010; Stephen Stills, Richie Furay, and Neil Young of Buffalo Springfield, June 11, 2011
SECOND ROW: Joss Stone, June 10, 2005; Julian Casablancas of the Strokes, June 12, 2011; Andrew Bird, June 14, 2009; Bo Bice and Trey Anastasio, June 11, 2005
THIRD ROW: Karen O of the Yeah Yeah Yeahs, June 12, 2009; Ray LaMontagne, June 10, 2011; Mumford and Sons, June 11, 2011; Bonnie Raitt, June 18, 2006; Taj Mahal, June 13, 2004
FOURTH ROW: Norah Jones, June 12, 2010; Lucinda Williams, June 13, 2003; Dave Rawlings, Conor Oberst, and Gillian Welch, June 16, 2006; Umphrey's McGee, June 12, 2005

NEXT PAGES: The White Stripes, June 17, 2007

THIS

"At some festivals in the past,
we've attempted to play only our
lighthearted material, but that's not
very representative, and if a festival
organizer has asked us to come and play,
we feel we should be ourselves—a little
bit over-the-top. So we'll try to make the
most inappropriate festival set possible,
and the funniest thing is, I think, often
it flies pretty well. People are so used to
seeing bands tailor their set list, with
the attitude 'Hey, everyone's having a
good time,' that it's refreshing to get
a little doom and gloom and some stuff
that requires an extra attention span."

—Colin Meloy, the Decemberists

"I can guarantee you that copies of this year's Bonnaroo program will be framed and put in every room of my house."

—Paul Meany, Mutemath

"I look forward to Bonnaroo because it's a chance for a band like us to break out of the bubble of our touring and the kind of show that we play. At Bonnaroo, you see different kinds of music and what people are enjoying—a lot of stuff that we wouldn't come across on our own. We get to walk by a stage and see anybody from GWAR to John Fogerty playing. Since we've been a band that grew up in a punk and hardcore scene, bringing our music to places where it might not be expected has always been a challenge. And that challenge is something that I thrive on and look forward to. I don't like playing shows in safe places where the response is predictable.

It's not often that Rise Against gets to anywhere in Tennessee, anywhere in the Southeast. These are different parts of the country and different kinds of people, which is all good. I'm looking forward to being in the midst of the hurricane that I'm sure Bonnaroo will be. I'd love to be able to absorb some of the culture that's happening down there. What's so exciting about a festival like Bonnaroo is that it's so diverse. Isis is playing across from Medeski Martin and Wood. If that's not the definition of diversity, I don't know what is."

—Tim McIlrath, Rise Against

ABOVE: Mutemath, June 14, 2007
BELOW: Rise Against, June 13, 2010

"Music fans danced in the sun and danced through a Saturday-night deluge here at the four-day Bonnaroo 2004 festival. What they danced to was virtually anything with—and sometimes without—a beat: bluegrass, heavy metal, funk, jazz, folk-rock, reggae, hip-hop, Indian tabla drumming, a New Orleans brass band, electronic noise and, for three hours Saturday night, the music of the festival's inspiration, the Dead. . . .

The music revolves around a benevolent sense of family that excludes no one. What matters is the feeling of connection: from past to present, from musician to musician, from style to style, from bands to fans. The North Mississippi Allstars, led by Luther and Cody Dickinson, brought friends and neighbors (the bluesman R. L. Burnside, the Rising Star Fife and Drum Band) as well as their father, Jim Dickinson. . . .

Bonnaroo was never purely a collection of jam bands, although this festival includes many circuit regulars. It favors bands that earn their living on the road, but nowadays those also include indie-rock bands, folk-rooted performers, and disc jockeys. Bonnaroo leans toward bands that savor the here-and-now of performing, with the volatile dynamics and improvisational serendipity that commercial recordings rarely capture."

—Jon Pareles, "A Family Feeling as the Bands Played On,"
New York Times, June 14, 2004

North Mississippi Allstars Hill Country
Revue, June 11, 2004

NEXT PAGES (clockwise from top left):
Crowd surfing, June 14, 2007;
Deadmau5, June 12, 2010; Public
Enemy, June 11, 2009; stage,
June 10, 2005

"People spoke about Bonnaroo with eyes more glowing than about most other festivals, so I expected some fig-leafed Xanadu. It ain't too far off, is it now, folks?"

—Elvis Perkins

"It was everything we thought it would be—times infinity."

—Evan Winiker, Steel Train

ABOVE: Elvis Perkins in Dearland, June 13, 2009
BELOW: Steel Train, June 17, 2006

"The audience loves to see something that happens only once that exact way. As a fan, I'm the same way."

—Warren Haynes, Gov't Mule

"I love congregations, and as church attendance subsides, festival attendance is on the increase. Maybe that's part of the new church system—people deciding that they want to be together and have a good time and celebrate life and music. And [musical] collaboration happens in a natural way, as soon as you pull people together. We like to be in bands, we like to play with folks, and surprises are always welcome, whether it's on the back porch or on the center stage of a festival. The exchange is a big part of music. And so let it carry on at Bonnaroo!"

—Daniel Lanois, Black Dub

FIRST ROW: Scissor Sisters, June 11, 2011; Tegan and Sara, June 13, 2008; Warren Haynes and Bob Weir with Gov't Mule, June 16, 2007
SECOND ROW: MGMT, June 12, 2008; Matt and Kim, June 10, 2011; Abigail Washburn, June 14, 2008; Ghostland Observatory, June 14, 2008; Daniel Lanois and Trixie Whitley of Black Dub, June 12, 2011
THIRD ROW: Vampire Weekend, June 12, 2008; Earl Scruggs, June 12, 2005; Passion Pit, June 11, 2009; Jakob Dylan, June 15, 2008; Dr. John, June 17, 2006
FOURTH ROW: Robyn Hitchcock and Peter Buck with the Venus 3, June 13, 2009; Grace Potter and the Nocturnals, June 12, 2009; James Blood Ulmer, June 15, 2007; Grizzly Bear, June 12, 2009

THAT

"There have been ten Bonnaroos, and I've been to nine of them. Aggregately, I have spent more than an entire month of my life in the freaky little town of Manchester, Tennessee. Most of the time, I've been at Bonnaroo on assignment, reporting for *Rolling Stone*, which means I've had good credentials and a hotel nearby, crucial to a city boy like me. The tens of thousands of people who sleep in the steaming tents are my heroes, basically. I will always marvel at the fortitude of the Bonnaroo fans. Even on Sunday, after being pummeled by days of heat, rain, and nonstop music, they still have the energy and the will to rock the fuck out. At Coachella and Lollapalooza, sometimes it's hard to even find a pulse.

Bonnaroo is such a singular experience that it can be difficult to sum up in a news story for *Rolling Stone*. With so many acts and so many distractions, the festival offers an infinite variety of ways to spend your weekend. In 2003, the first year I went, I was running around like a madman trying to get the scoop. I was adhering to my predetermined itinerary of shows and interviewing so many bands that it was hard to relax and settle in. All I remember now of that inaugural festival is playing golf with Ween on the second floor of the Holiday Inn Express. It was three A.M., we had a five iron, a putter, and a plastic beer cup, and there was money on the line. I'll never forget that.

I've had so many bizarre experiences over the years at Bonnaroo that my memories of the festival have coalesced into a hazy jumble. There are dozens of musical moments that stand out, for sure: Bob Dylan playing 'Blind Willie McTell' on the main stage; Kanye West performing as the sun rose in Tennessee; LCD Soundsystem's late-night set; Levon Helm singing 'King Harvest'; Eddie Vedder sharing his bottle of red wine with the front row; My Morning Jacket's puppet show on the Which Stage; Stevie Wonder's heroic set; Mars Volta playing most of *Frances the Mute*, etc. I've also taken personal pride in seeing friends like the Black Keys and Kings of Leon go from tents to the top of the bill. And like summer camp, Bonnaroo follows no script.

What may be most memorable are the things that go down in between the music: scarfing down crack-of-dawn All-Star Specials at Waffle House; making the inevitable run to Walmart for rain gear; devouring an entire pig with the Kings of Leon; seeing Kareem Abdul-Jabbar backstage; trying to make out with a girl on the Ferris wheel; going on the adult slip 'n' slide; and having marathon conversations where every verb is replaced with the word 'Roo.' These random elements make Bonnaroo the only festival I look forward to each and every summer.

After a few years of hearing me rave about Bonnaroo, I finally dragged my friends at *Rolling Stone* down to Tennessee. Not long after, *Rolling Stone* declared Bonnaroo the best festival in America, and subsequently one of the '50 moments that changed the history of rock and roll.' I'm proud to have played a part in that. I'm also proud to say that after nearly a decade, I have become ever so slightly more tolerant of people who choose to play hacky-sack. Long live Bonnaroo!"

—Austin Scaggs
music writer, *Rolling Stone*

PREVIOUS PAGES: M.I.A.,
June 13, 2008

LEFT: Dillinger Escape Plan,
June 14, 2009

"The best time I had at Bonnaroo was in 2009. We decided to go into the campgrounds. I'd never done that before at the festival, so my friends and I just wandered deep, deep, deep, and all of a sudden it's like you're in this whole other world that, I would guess, a lot of artists don't get to experience. There's a lot of music happening, and it's a social place, and people are doing everything you can imagine.

We ended up spending three hours just wandering and hanging out and meeting people, and even running into people who had seen me play the day before. They were naturally a little bit surprised that we were two miles deep into the campground. That was the best time I've ever had just actually chilling out on that level. Which I think says a lot about the nature of the festival. The social component is huge, and obviously music is a big part of it, or the focus of it, and that's what makes or breaks the festival. But at the same time, that social dynamic is what makes it something beyond a show. That's what makes it a festival."

—Gregg Gillis, Girl Talk

Girl Talk, June 12, 2009

NEXT PAGES: Mastodon, June 14, 2008;
Cage the Elephant, June 14, 2009

"Del McCoury's bus broke down outside of Chicago at three A.M. following our American Legacies gig. Preservation Hall [Jazz Band] turned around, picked up the stranded McCourys on the side of the highway in the snow. Once aboard the bus, Ronnie McCoury presented the idea that the two groups work together to create an original Bonnaroo theme song in celebration of the tenth-year anniversary [of Del McCoury's performance at the first-ever Bonnaroo]. The melody and lyrics came to Preservation Hall vocalist Clint Maedgen as if the song had already been written. An hour later, the first version of 'Bonnaroo (Feel the Magic)' was recorded on an iPhone, and a video was recorded backstage the following night."

—Ben Jaffe, Preservation Hall Jazz Band

"Bonnaroo (Feel the Magic)"

Bonnaroo, Bonnaroo, Bonnaroo
Feel the magic in the air
Bonnaroo, Bonnaroo, Bonnaroo
Feel the magic everywhere . . .
They're having a good time
Counting down the miles before we cross
that state line to lose these blues
Bonnaroo me and you
Tennessee Bonnaroo

"It takes a lot to stand out in a crowd so big. For example, the Bonnaroo Band-to-Be in 2011 was Preservation Hall Jazz Band, who popped up to play on various stages with My Morning Jacket; Ben Sollee; Dr. John, the Meters, and Allen Toussaint; and Del McCoury, and then led a late-night parade on a Mr. T float through the festival grounds to an unannounced show with Portugal.The Man. I bet even Warren Haynes would be impressed!"

—Rita Houston, program director, WFUV, New York, NY

The Preservation Hall Jazz Band and the
Del McCoury Band, June 11, 2011

"I've visited Bonnaroo twice: once with Allen Toussaint, the Imposters, and Crescent City Horns; and a couple of years later 'solo,' although I was joined onstage by A.T., Jim Lauderdale, and Jenny Lewis and her players for a couple of numbers each. Those two experiences are good bookends that illustrate the virtues of the event.

The tent show was a riot. I like playing solo but got a lot of help from the crowd on the tunes they knew. Allen Toussaint played piano and sang with me on 'Who's Gonna Help Brother Get Further?' and 'The River in Reverse'; Jim Lauderdale came up for a few tunes, including 'Femme Fatale' and 'Sulphur to Sugarcane'; and Jenny Lewis arrived for 'The Crooked Line.' I'd jumped up for 'Carpetbaggers' at the end of her set, so Jenny, [Jonathan] Rice, Farmer Dave, and others arrived for the closing rock 'n' roll finale on 'Go Away' and 'Peace, Love and Understanding.' I suppose that kind of happy crew is what Bonnaroo is all about."

—Elvis Costello

Jenny Lewis with Elvis Costello,
June 13, 2009

"It's always a trip going back in a time zone, but we had tried to approach [performing *Desitively Bonnaroo*] some fresh ways, without looking at it going backways. That's what music's about. We were doing the best we could. With the little bit of time we had to woodshed on it, I think we did OK. It was cool that we had Allen there, we had the Meters, we had the girls singing—everything we could do to try to recaptivate what was, yet still trying to be loose with it and keep it current. It's always good to communicate. It don't matter to what age bracket—it's really not what music's about. As Louis Armstrong and Duke Ellington once said, 'There's only two kinds of music, good and bad.' And that makes it simple."

—Dr. John, on reuniting with the original Meters and Allen Toussaint to play their 1974 album *Desitively Bonnaroo* live for the first time

"Trying to come up with a name for the festival we'd conceived, we started flipping through our record collections. We came across Dr. John's *Desitively Bonnaroo*. The word 'Bonnaroo' immediately jumped out at us. Given our New Orleans roots and the definition (creole slang for 'good stuff'), we knew we had our name."

—Jonathan Mayers, Superfly Presents

The Meters, Dr. John, and Allen Toussaint, June 11, 2011

NEXT PAGES (clockwise from top left): Deertick, June 11, 2011; the XX, June 10, 2010; the Black Keys, June 15, 2007; the Black Angels, June 10, 2011

"One of the best moments of the SuperJam for me was during our rehearsal. We were getting the backing vocals together for 'I Walk on Gilded Splinters.' Mac [Dr. John] told us the lyrics on the refrain are *Corn boule killy caw caw.* As we were noting that, Dan [Auerbach] asked, 'What's that mean?' We all leaned in with great anticipation to learn the secret, and Mac said in his low, cool voice, 'It means cornbread, coffee, and molasses.' It was psychedelic."

—Brian Olive

LEFT: Steve Martin, June 11, 2010

ABOVE: SuperJam '11: Dan Auerbach and Dr. John (center) surrounded by members of the Preservation Hall Jazz Band, Patrick Hallahan of My Morning Jacket (far right), and other participants, June 12, 2011

"We started playing Bonnaroo in 2005, came three years ago, and now we're back [in 2011]. I brought my kids with me for the first time—that was a lot of fun. That was the first big outdoor festival I ever played, so it was a big deal for me personally. The first time we came to Bonnaroo, I think we had five people [in the band], then the next time it was eight, and this time it's either eleven or twelve, with a horn section and some backing vocals."

—Sam Beam, Iron and Wine

"During year one, Old Crow Medicine Show's manager asked me if I cared if the band busked in my press area. I thought it was a great idea and they killed it! Such a great band. And it made for the best gift to the press. So I was inspired then and there to do this every year for the journalists, and now I book a band to perform in the press tent every Saturday. In 2003, I booked the Polyphonic Spree. They had just finished performing in That Tent. I walked up there and went backstage to gather the band and proceeded to march them across Centeroo to my press tent. There I was, leading a procession of twenty-five people in white robes across Bonnaroo. I felt like the Pied Piper, Jim Jones. Those voices, those songs, that tent. It was amazing."

—Ken Weinstein, president, Big Hassle Media

ABOVE: Sam Beam of Iron and Wine, June 11, 2005
BELOW: The Polyphonic Spree, June 14, 2003

NEXT PAGES: FIRST ROW: Sonic Youth, June 13, 2003; Shadows Fall, June 14, 2009; Charlie Louvin, June 17, 2007; Yeasayer, June 13, 2009; the Black Keys, June 11, 2004; Kris Kristofferson, June 13, 2010; Devendra Banhart, June 16, 2006
SECOND ROW: Deerhunter, June 9, 2011; Solomon Burke, June 15, 2008; Colonel Claypool's Bucket of Bernie Brains, June 22, 2002; the Low Anthem, June 11, 2011; Loretta Lynn, June 11, 2011; Patti Smith, June 11, 2004; St. Vincent, June 12, 2009
THIRD ROW: Robert Randolph, June 23, 2002; Mr. Lif of the Perceptionists, June 11, 2005; the XX, June 10, 2010; Fiery Furnaces, June 13, 2008; fans, June 10, 2010; Neon Indian, June 10, 2010; Langhorne Slim, June 12, 2010
FOURTH ROW: Local Natives, June 10, 2010, St. Vincent, June 12, 2009; !!!, June 13, 2008; Santigold, June 12, 2009; Deerhunter, June 9, 2011; Crystal Castles, June 12, 2009; Allen Toussaint, June 11, 2011; Local Natives, June 10, 2010

THE

OTHER

"I'm grateful for this audience. I'm the first Italian playing here. The most important people from the world are playing here. For me, as an Italian artist, being here is something important. In Italy, it's in the newspaper and on the television.

In these three days, you can have a life-changing experience. In general, if you go to concerts, you'll see lots of people with cell phones and small cameras. But here you won't see people messaging, because they want to be in the moment. Usually when I'm onstage, I'll see flashes in front of me for two hours. Here they don't have this kind of strange fever, because they don't need it. Bonnaroo is sort of primitive, spiritual, sensual. You will never forget."

—Jovanotti

PREVIOUS PAGES: Sleigh Bells, June 9, 2011

LEFT: Jovanotti, June 11, 2011

RIGHT: Bootsy Collins and the Funk University, June 11, 2011

"Wanda Jackson, we worship the ground you rock on!"

—Kendall Morgan, fan, Nashville, TN

"My granddaughter and her friend had been coming to Bonnaroo from Oklahoma for several years; they save all year so that they can go. They camp out and get the whole experience, and they just dearly love it. For a couple of years they've been telling me I should do that show, like I could just call up and say, 'I want to do it'—it doesn't work that way. But finally, this year I was invited to be a part of it, and they were thrilled, and I was thrilled, knowing it was the biggest one in America. Then my experience when I got there was wonderful. Everything was organized beautifully, I was well taken care of and picked up and taken right to the stage, and I had a nice dressing room, and the people were wonderful and helpful. Then when I went onstage, I couldn't see any of the audience except just a few around the sides, so I was hoping that I had a crowd—I didn't really have any idea. When I stepped out—my goodness, there must have been thousands. And they were listening to every word. They were a very courteous, interested, and lively audience, so as a performer, you can't ask for more. Their energy and waves of love—I just feel those waves coming at me from them, and it's wonderful. Yeah, it's addictive, really."

—Wanda Jackson

Wanda Jackson, June 10, 2011

NEXT PAGES (clockwise from top left): GWAR, June 12, 2010; John Paul Jones, ?uestlove, and Ben Harper, June 15, 2007; Ratatat, June 10, 2011; Edward Sharpe & the Magnetic Zeros, June 11, 2010

"The excitement and joy of discovering great new music is at the heart of the Bonnaroo experience. One of the tremendous pleasures of booking the festival is sharing some of the wonderful music that we've discovered that may be a bit off the radar for many fans. We've done this from the beginning. But the idea of themed or curated tents emerged from wanting to create a context that enhances the presentation of these artists during the festival weekend. (And it's fun, too.)

It started with the Cabaret tent during the early festival days, which then evolved into the jazz club one year, and then there was a New Orleans club the following year. But it really became fully developed when we created the African tent in 2009. That was amazing—a 'who's who' of some of Africa's greatest musicians. It was its own fantastic festival within the bigger festival. I know people who say they spent their entire day there.

The Latino tent the following year was equally fabulous, hosted and curated by Ozomatli, with some of the hottest contemporary bands from South America. And then in 2011, I was able to enlist Eugene Hütz from Gogol Bordello to create the Gypsy Punk World Mash-Up tent, which included artists from Mongolia, Italy, Syria, Brazil, and beyond—complete with some crazy wonderful once-in-a-lifetime collaborations. It was unforgettable.

While I love programming the tents myself, I find it especially rewarding to collaborate with guest curators like Eugene Hütz and David Byrne. I love the process because it leads me to discover all sorts of new music or to sometimes hear music that I thought I knew in a whole new way. And it opens up more and more exciting ideas for future Bonnaroos. The possibilities are endless."

—Ashley Capps, AC Entertainment

ABOVE: Femi Kuti and the Positive Force, June 12, 2009
BELOW: Toumani Diabaté, June 12, 2009

RIGHT: Amadou and Mariam, June 12, 2009

"Daryl Hall and Chromeo was a hallmark Bonnaroo moment. We paired up two artists who had never performed live together. My original idea was to have Daryl play his set and then have Chromeo sit in for a few songs, with Chromeo continuing with their own set. They were both so excited about the project that they decided to learn each other's songs and do the whole show together. The tragedy is that we did not end up taping the performance, but in a way it is almost fitting, as it is one of those great moments that will live on only with the people who were there."

—Kerry Black, Superfly Presents

Daryl Hall and Chromeo, June 20, 2010

Galactic, June 11, 2010

"Hopefully, we'll be educating young fans about New Orleans music and how great it is. It's been around for a long time and will be around for a lot longer."

—Robert Mercurio, Galactic

"We're programming what our music collections are. When you look at what people have in their iPods, it's everything from hip-hop to indie rock to jazz to folk—a million different things. That's where our programming concept comes from."

—Rick Farman, Superfly Presents

FIRST ROW: Amanda Palmer of the Dresden Dolls, June 17, 2006; Brian Viglione of the Dresden Dolls, June 17, 2006; Bettye LaVette, June 16, 2006; Nicole Atkins, June 12, 2011; Ralph Stanley, June 17, 2007
SECOND ROW: Ben Sollee, June 10, 2011; Adele, June 13, 2008; Steve Earle, June 18, 2006; the Knux, June 11, 2009
THIRD ROW: Ornette Coleman, June 17, 2007; Ted Leo and the Pharmacists, June 14, 2009; Lotus, June 10, 2010; fans, June 10, 2010; Janelle Monáe, June 11, 2009
FOURTH ROW: Gogol Bordello, June 11, 2011; Hanggai, June 11, 2011; Robyn, June 12, 2011; Big Boi, June 10, 2011

COMEDY

"I dove into the crowd at my show and suddenly realized that no one had bathed in four days. It was a strange combination of erotic and disgusting."

—Conan O'Brien

"Bonnaroo seems very laid back. That is what is so wonderful about it. It does not seem aggressive. Bonnaroo is like that old, kind, rednecky uncle who is also a hippie who just likes to sit back and make music and smoke up some dreams."

—Zach Galifianakis

Conan O'Brien, June 12, 2010

NEXT PAGES (clockwise from top left): Zach Galifianakis, June 12, 2008; Chris Rock, June 13, 2008; Fred Armisen, June 10, 2005; Louis C.K., June 15, 2008

"...You Might Be a Deadneck"

If you beat yourself up because you're a dirty hippie, you might be a deadneck.

If you live in a rural town below the Mason-Dixon line and you happen to listen to a lot of Widespread Panic, you might be a deadneck.

If you have a bumper sticker that says, "America: Love it AND leave it," you might be a deadneck.

If you actively oppose gay marriage, you live in a red state below the Mason-Dixon line, and you happen to like the String Cheese Incident a lot, you might be a deadneck.

If you hacky sack, but only with white people, you might be a deadneck.

If your favorite pastime is listening to "Sugar Magnolia" while watching *Steel Magnolias*, then you might be a deadneck.

If you're really into dipping, and by dipping you mean putting your hand in a CD crate full of Ben Harper CDs, you might be a deadneck.

If you smell like shit, you might be a deadneck.

—David Cross, Aziz Ansari, and Nick Kroll

ABOVE: Nick Kroll, June 14, 2007

RIGHT ABOVE: David Cross,
June 14, 2007
RIGHT BELOW: Aziz Ansari,
June 14, 2007

"I used to be a hippie, so Bonnaroo is easy. I love wandering around in the midst of everybody. It basically vindicates all the feelings I've had my whole life. And if I'd stayed in Chapel Hill, North Carolina, I'd still be dressed like a hippie."

—Lewis Black

LEFT: Jimmy Fallon, June 13, 2009

ABOVE: Lewis Black, June 9, 2011

"If I were the producer of Bonnaroo, I'd hold it in the desert in Needles, California, in the summer. . . . All the security guards would be on parole or work release from prison, and their friends—since we have your addresses from when you ordered your tickets— would be robbing your homes."

—John Waters

"While music is the core to the festival's programming, other mini festivals and attractions have emerged underneath the Bonnaroo umbrella: a comedy festival, a film festival, a craft beer festival, and art installations. There's something for everyone, and no two people have the same experience."

—Jonathan Mayers, Superfly Presents

"My original motivation to head toward the comedy tent was to escape the heat, and, true, the air-conditioning and comfy seats were a huge draw. But the sardonic storytelling and sick humor of John Waters became one of the highlights of my weekend."

—George Holland, fan, Asheboro, NC

Bonnaroo Glossary by Funny or Die

Over the years, Bonnaroo has developed a language all its own. Here are some terms that may help you have a better trip.

Bonna-rookie — A first-timer.

Bonna-rager — When you party real hard at Bonnaroo.

Bonnar-oops! There it is! — A celebratory chant used by frat boys at the festival.

Tenne-C-section — When you're such a dick at Bonnaroo that you not only get kicked out of the festival, you're asked to leave the state.

Bob Gnarley — A guy (or girl) who dresses like a hippie but acts like white trash.

Poopay Fiasco — A disastrous port-a-potty situation.

Death Cab on the QT — When someone who came to see Metallica, the Sword, and Mastodon sneaks off to an indie rock show and doesn't want their friends to know about it.

Janeane Garofalowdown — When someone who came to see Drive-By Truckers sneaks off to see an alternative political comic and doesn't want their friends to know about it.

Ladytron Dong — You meet a sexy robot and start to fool around, and when you reach into her robot panties there's a big ol' metal dick in there.

Chris Rock in a Hard Place — Chris Rock and a band you really like are performing at the same time and you have to make a difficult decision.

My Morning Jacket Hoodie — A confusing piece of merchandise.

Ben Folds — Bonnaroo's on-site laundry service.

Robert Plant — A factory where all the Bobs are made.

Phil Lesh — Opposite of John Tesh.

Israel Vibrator — A sex toy for Jewish hippies.

Yonder Mountain String Ban — No more string on that mountain over there.

Lez Zeppelin — Rosie O'Donnell.

Cat Power — What Lez Zeppelin runs on.

Disco Biscuits — The food that made John Travolta fat and gross.

Roo-Doo — Good or bad luck at a music festival, i.e., "I've got some really good roo-doo today!"

Willie Full-Nelson — A wrestling move used by awesome country singers.

FIRST ROW: Jim Norton, June 14, 2008; Rob Riggle, June 13, 2009; Margaret Cho, June 11, 2010; J.B. Smoove, June 10, 2010
SECOND ROW: Bo Burnham, June 13, 2010; Cheech Marin, June 9, 2011; Doug Benson, June 13, 2010; Reggie Watts, June 13, 2008; Greg Giraldo, June 13, 2010
THIRD ROW: John Oliver, June 13, 2009; Kristen Schaal and Kurt Braunohler, June 14, 2009; John Mulaney, June 13, 2008; Robert Smigel and Triumph the Insult Comic Dog, June 12, 2009; Janeane Garofalo, June 11, 2009
FOURTH ROW: Demetri Martin, June 17, 2007; Mike Birbiglia, June 13, 2008; the Gregory Brothers, June 12, 2011; Jeffrey Ross, June 11, 2010; Henry Rollins, June 9, 2011

CINEMA

ABOVE: D. A. Pennebaker,
June 14, 2007

RIGHT ABOVE: Cinema tent,
June 11, 2011
RIGHT BELOW: Jim Jarmusch,
June 17, 2007

"We have always strived to show our connection to New Orleans, and the parade is a special part of Bonnaroo, especially for the staff. We started it the first year and built two floats, Mr. T and a dragon. We made Bonnaroo branded beads and doubloons and had a brass band lead the parade. Various staff and friends would ride the float and throw the beads. In 2004 we hired William Hung [at right, second photo from top] to ride the float with us and then perform at the end of the parade. We went through the campgrounds and ended in Centeroo; there were thousands of people who flocked to the float and went nuts when Hung belted out his famous rendition of Ricky Martin's 'She Bangs.' His mother was there with him the whole time to keep an eye on him. As he descended from the float, there was a line of people waiting to talk to him. The following year we did the same thing with Bo Bice, who also ended up sitting in with Trey Anastasio. After a few years off, we resurrected the parade in 2011 as a walking parade led by the Preservation Hall Jazz Band, which started after Dr. John and the Meters performed *Desitively Bonnaroo*. Members of My Morning Jacket also paraded with us as we marched to the bottom of Centeroo, where Portugal. The Man was waiting to play a surprise show from a refurbished Mr. T float."

—Kerry Black, Superfly Presents

"There is a sense of surprise and discovery wherever I walk around the site."

—Ashley Capps, AC Entertainment

PARADE

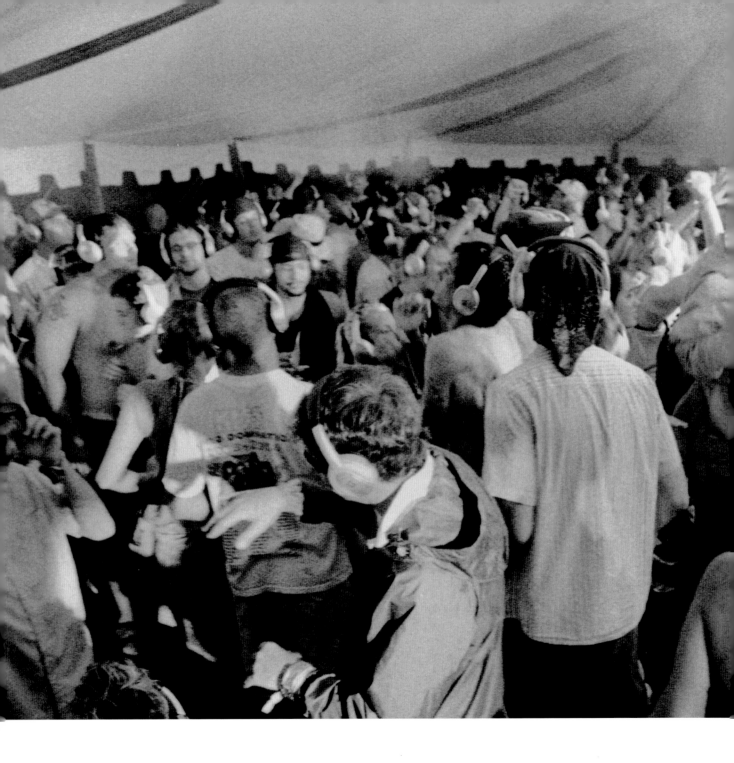

SILENT DISCO

"When you first see the Silent Disco, it takes a minute to register what's going on in there. Then, it's completely delightful. Like watching a hundred people dancing alone in their apartments. That kind of 'concentrating on the music, not worrying about anything' dancing people do when they aren't being watched. Except here, everybody was smiling at everybody else. Just walking by the tent, watching everybody throw their arms in the air, or hopping up and down—it was impossible not to smile along."

—Kate Moloney, fan, Brooklyn, NY

"The Silent Disco was such a new concept. It was odd to be wandering around with music and ambient sound everywhere and come upon the 'deaf tent,' with people wearing headphones dancing like crazy to music we couldn't hear. It was like a vacuum or black hole among the hullabaloo."

—Mimi Goese, fan, New York, NY

ETC

DANNY'S

PHOTO BOOTH

"Neil Young doesn't necessarily like to sit for photographs; he doesn't like to do press. I've gotten a rapport with Neil in the past couple of years that I'm really proud of because he's one of my end-all heroes. In 2003, I was thinking, 'I've got to get Neil into my portrait studio.' He was in the catering tent, and I saw him start to stir, and he comes out and I'm walking toward him and I say, sarcastically, 'Neil, I know you love having your picture taken. You think you'd want to come over and have your official Bonnaroo photograph taken in my portrait area?' And he says, 'Oh, geez, alright. Make me look good, Danny.' And I notice he's got a paper plate in his hand from catering, and on the paper plate is his set list, which he wrote on the plate while eating dinner. So he's got these badass wraparound sunglasses on, and I have him holding the set list on a plate. That ranks up there as one of my favorites."

—Danny Clinch

"You're waiting for that moment, and you have to hone your skills for knowing when that moment's going to come. It's anticipation, which becomes instinct after a while."

—Danny Clinch

James Hetfield, June 13, 2008

NEXT PAGES (clockwise from top left): Michael Franti and Ziggy Marley, June 15, 2007; Gillian Welch and Dave Rawlings, June 11, 2004; the Raconteurs, June 13, 2008

"Bonnaroo is one big amusement park, where we are supplying them with entertainment. It feels great to just vibe off everyone."

—DJ Logic

DJ Logic, June 12, 2002

RIGHT: Bruce Springsteen,
June 13, 2009

"Getting this photograph of Jeff Tweedy and Bob Dylan together was epic. It's nothing but a simple document, but it's two musicians together who I admire."

—Danny Clinch

"When we played Bonnaroo, we got such a nice vibe—a genuine good feeling from the first beat. Things like Bonnaroo give you the hope that you can do it the other way…. It's great. I dream to take some of that vibe and take it around the country."

—Thom Yorke, Radiohead

"I've noticed at this festival that back-stage all the musicians dig hanging out together. Everybody talks. Everyone's excited to see the band that plays after them."

—Jack Johnson

PREVIOUS PAGES: Bob Dylan and Jeff
Tweedy, June 11, 2004; Radiohead,
June 17, 2006

LEFT: Jack Johnson and Eddie
Vedder, June 14, 2008

ABOVE: Beck (center) with his band and
(at far right) Thom Yorke, June 17, 2006

NEXT PAGES: James Brown, June 15,
2003

"Bonnaroo 2006 was my first 'Roo experience. It was a graduation gift from my mom. Bonnaroo is not just a music and arts festival; it's a life-altering experience, a way of life that nobody can fully grasp unless they have been there. There are so many things in life that can get you down, but there is a place in Manchester, Tennessee, where you can let go of all the negative and rejoice in the positive, simple things in life: music, laughter, compassion, and love. Since my first year, my mom and I have made a promise to return to Bonnaroo every year. Hard times come and go, but we always try to save the money for a ticket because it's the one place we are free to be ourselves and enjoy the music that has enriched our lives for so many years."

—Betsy Ward, fan, Lyman, SC

"I was so sad when Bonnaroo was over. When I got home, I ran to the grocery store to buy a pint of Ben & Jerry's Bonnaroo Buzz ice cream. I'd heard that coffee ice cream was chosen because the festival is located in Coffee County. And the whiskey flavor is a nod to the whiskey distillery nearby. When I'm feeling homesick for Bonnaroo, at least I know the ice cream is only a few blocks away!"

—Tamar Brazis, fan, New York, NY

"In 2002 I attended the first Bonnaroo Music and Arts Festival. I was twenty-five years old and struggling to find my place in the world. Bonnaroo changed all of that. On the last night of the festival, watching Widespread Panic's Mikey Houser wail away on his guitar in what would become one of the last concerts he ever played on this earth, I realized that life is short and unexpected, and that only by doing what I loved would I find true happiness."

—Charles M. Bell, fan, Morrisville, NC

POSTERS

2002 poster designed by Vance Kelly

NEXT PAGES: FIRST ROW: 2003 poster designed by Mike King; 2004 poster designed by Jager DiPaola Kemp Design; 2005 poster designed by Kari Roberts Petsche; 2006 poster designed by Mike Davis for Burlesque of North America; 2007 poster designed by Ames Bros SECOND ROW: 2008 poster designed by Steven Wilson, www.breedlondon.com; 2009 and 2010 posters designed by Mike Davis for Burlesque of North America; 2011 poster designed by Pat Perry

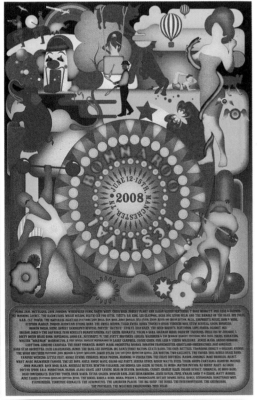

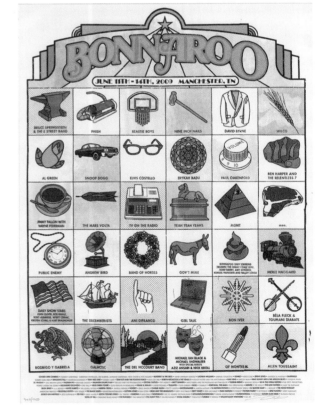

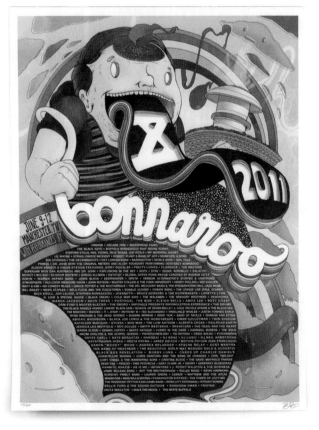

Just as it takes a team of hardworking, creative people to put together a festival like Bonnaroo, so did numerous folks lend a hand to make this book happen. A million thanks to the following: all those at Superfly Presents and AC Entertainment, especially Kerry Black, Rick Farman, Ashley Capps, Jon Mayers, Coran Capshaw, and Rich Goodstone, as well as Robin McNicol, Laura Gentry Carter, and Russ Bennett; our editor Tamar Brazis and the team at Abrams, Jenna Pocius, David Blatty, Steve Tager, Deb Aaronson, Liam Flanagan, and Danny Maloney; our literary agents Sarah Lazin and Carol Mann; Big Hassle's Ken Weinstein and his crew; the artists who gave us their thoughts on 'Roo, including Dr. John, Elvis Costello, Thomas Mars, Conan O'Brien, Zach Galifianakis, David Cross, Patterson Hood, Wanda Jackson, Jovanotti, Ben Sollee, Brian Olive, Eugene Hütz, Ben Folds, Jim James, Patrick Hallahan, Stewart Copeland, Aaron Dessner, Matisyahu, Nick Harmer, Colin Meloy, Tim McIlrath, Daniel Lanois, Phil Lesh, Greg Gillis, David Byrne, Sam Beam, Lewis Black, Mike McCready, Ben Harper, Lars Ulrich, Steven Van Zandt, Nathan Followill, and Mike Gordon; Alan Light, whose many contributions were essential to the book; the writers who shared their own interviews and insights, Jesse Jarnow, Tim Donnelly, Austin Scaggs, Jon Pareles, John Barry, Mike Greenhaus, Josh Baron, Dean Budnick, Emily Zemler, Rita Houston, and Alison Fensterstock; the photographers and those who enable them, Ryan Mastro, Danny Clinch, Jeff Levine, Lisa Connolly, Josh Goleman, C. Taylor Crothers, Adam Macchia, Morgan Harris, Doug Mason, Jeff Kravitz and those at Film Magic, Taylor Hill, Michael Loccisano, and Jason Merritt; designers Ellen Nygaard, Justin Krietemeyer, and Steve Harrington; and all those others who helped in ways large and small, among them, Joe Ford, Robert Warren, Rocky Benloulou-Duben, Peter Himberger, David Pennington, Betty Superstein, David Whitehead, Mimi Goese, Judy Whitfield, Quinn Ferris, Kate Moloney, and Antoine Wagner. Finally, many thanks to the artists who've played Bonnaroo and can be seen in these pages, and especially to the fans—particularly those who shared their stories and images and inspired us as we created this book.

—Holly George-Warren

THANK YOU

We'd like to express our deepest appreciation to all of those who made this book possible: To our incredible, creative, and unwavering Bonnaroo team who continue to dedicate themselves to creating a fantastic music festival year after year, and who have brought that dedication to this endeavor. To Coran Capshaw for believing in the festival when it was just an idea, and for his unwavering support and thoughtful guidance. To the residents of Manchester and Coffee County, Tennessee, who have graciously welcomed us to and made us a part of their community. To all the wonderful musicians, artists, and comedians whose work continues to provide the inspiration and excitement for Bonnaroo—a special thanks to those who contributed their insights and memories to the printed page. To those who envisioned this book and helped us put it together, including Carol Mann, Tamar Brazis, Holly George-Warren, Alan Light, Justin Krietemeyer, Steve Harrington, Ellen Nygaard, Robin McNicol, Laura Gentry Carter, and Rocky Benloulou-Dubin. To the extremely talented and hardworking photographers whose evocative images are showcased here: Danny Clinch, C. Taylor Crothers, Morgan Harris, Taylor Hill, Jeff Kravitz, Michael Loccisano, Adam Macchia, Doug Mason, Ryan Mastro, and Jason Merritt. And, especially, to all of you who have attended Bonnaroo over the past decade and shared your bountiful spirit and enthusiasm. We thank you for making Bonnaroo the amazing experience that it is for all of us, and for encouraging us to document it with this book.

—Superfly Presents and AC Entertainment

Danny Clinch: 40, 54-55, 58-59, 76, 82-83, 90 [bottom], 95 [3rd row, 5], 96-97, 108 [top], 125, 132-133, 166, 171, 173 [top], 174-175 [3rd row, 1], 185 [top], 196, 199 [bottom], 201 [bottom], 208, 209 [bottom], 214-215 [3rd row, 8], 216-217, 219, 220-221, 222, 223, 224, 225, 226, 227, 228, 229, 230-231

C. Taylor Crothers: 6, 7, 8, 9, 12, 18 [top], 20, 24, 27 [1st row, 2, 5; 2nd row, 3; 3rd row, 4; 5th row, 1, 4], 35, 43 [bottom], 47 [1st row, 2, 3; 3rd row, 1, 4; 4th row, 2, 3], 48-49, 53, 54, 56, 62-63, 68 [top], 73, 85, 86, 87, 88, 89, 95 [1st row, 1, 2, 5; 2nd row, 1, 4; 3rd row, 4th row, 3, 4], 102-103, 104 [bottom 2], 106, 109 [bottom], 116, 117, 118, 119, 122, 126 [bottom], 129 [top], 131 [1st row, 1, 2, 5; 2nd row, all; 3rd row, 1, 2; 4th row, 2, 3], 144, 146 [bottom], 148 [top], 151 [1st row, 1; 2nd row, 1, 3; 3rd row, 1, 2, 3, 4; 4th row, 2, 3], 165, 169 [bottom], 170, 172 [bottom], 174-175 [1st row, 1, 5; 3rd row, 2; 4th row, 4], 193 [4th row, 1, 3], 207 [1st row, 3, 4; 2nd row, 2; 4th row, 5], 210 [top, 2nd from bottom], 211 [top], 214-215 [1st row, 1, 2, 8; 2nd row, 1, 6, 8; 3rd row, 6],

Adam Dubin: 200

Film Magic:

    Taylor Hill: 147 [top], 151 [2nd row, 5], 186 [top], 204, 207 [1st row, 2; 3rd row, 1, 2, 5; 4th row, 3]

    Jason Kempin: 174-175 [1st row, 7]

    Jeff Kravitz: 43 [top], 44, 52-53, 57 [top, center], 61, 64, 71 [top], 80, 95 [1st row, 3; 2nd row, 3, 5; 4th row, 1], 100-101, 105, 112-113, 114, 126 [top], 131 [1st row, 3; 3rd row, 3, 4, 5; 4th row, 4], 151 [4th row, 1], 174-175 [2nd row, 3], 214-215 [3rd row, 2, 7]

    Michael Loccisano: 159, 174-175 [1st row, 3], 187, 201 [top]

    Jason Merritt: 90 [top], 151 [1st row, 3; 3rd row, 5], 174-175 [2nd row, 2, 6], 193 [1st row, 1, 2, 3, 5; 2nd row, 2, 3; 3rd row, 1], 207 [1st row, 1; 2nd row, 3; 4th row, 1, 4], 210 [2nd from top; 4th from top]

    Anna Webber: 174-175 [2nd row, 5]

    Misc.: 203, 206 [2nd row, 1,4; 3rd row, 3]

Laura Grunfeld: 47 [3rd row, 5]

Morgan Harris: 188, 189, 193 [3rd row, 4], 207 [2nd row, 5], 213 [bottom row]

Adam Macchia: 6, 7, 8, 9, 10, 19 [bottom], 27 [1st row, 3, 4; 2nd row, 1, 2, 5; 3rd row, 1, 2, 3; 4th row, 1, 2, 3, 4; 5th row, 2, 3; 6th row, 1, 2, 4], 32, 39, 47 [2nd row, 1, 4; 3rd row, 2, 3; 4th row, 4], 95 [3rd row, 2], 107 [top 2], 147 [bottom], 151 [2nd row, 2; 4th row, 4], 169 [top], 174-175 [1st row, 2, 4, 6; 2nd row, 1, 7; 3rd row, 3, 5, 6, 7; 4th row, 1, 2, 5, 6], 186 [bottom], 193 [1st row, 4; 2nd row, 1; 3rd row, 2; 4th row, 2, 4], 202, 209 [bottom], 213 [top right], 214-215 [2nd row, 3, 4, 7]

Douglas Mason: 14-15, 27 [2nd row, 4], 36-37, 68 [bottom], 92-93, 95 [2nd row, 2; 3rd row, 1, 3], 107 [bottom], 129 [bottom], 131 [1st row, 4], 193 [2nd row, 4; 3rd row, 5], 210 [bottom], 213 [top left], 214-215 [1st row, 6; 2nd row, 2; 3rd row, 4, 5], 237

Ryan Mastro: 6 [center, far left; bottom, far left], 7 [center, far right], 16-17, 21, 22, 23, 27 [3rd row, 5; 5th row, 5, 6th row, 3], 28, 30-31, 33, 38, 47 [1st row, 1, 4; 2nd row, 1, 3; 4th row, 1], 50-51, 57 [bottom], 65, 66-67, 70, 71 [bottom], 74-75, 78, 79, 84, 95 [1st row, 4; 4th row, 2], 98-99, 104 [top 2], 108 [bottom], 109 [top], 110, 111, 115, 121, 131 [4th row, 1], 134-135, 136-137, 138, 139, 140, 141, 143, 146 [bottom], 148 [bottom], 151 [1st row, 2, 2nd row, 4], 152-153, 154-155, 156, 158, 160, 161, 162-163, 167, 168, 174-175 [2nd row, 4; 3rd row, 4; 4th row, 3, 7, 8], 176-177, 178-179, 180, 181, 182, 184, 185 [bottom], 190-191, 193 [3rd row, 3], 194-195, 198, 199 [top], 207 [3rd row, 4; 5th row, 2], 210 [3rd from top], 211 [bottom], 212, 214-215 [1st row, 3, 5, 7; 2nd row, 5; 3rd row, 1, 3], 239

David Whitehead: 214-215 [1st row, 4]

PHOTO CREDITS

EDITOR: Tamar Brazis
DESIGNER: National Forest
PRODUCTION MANAGER: Jacquie Poirier

Cover photography credits: Background photo (sky) and top two photos (arch and fountain) by Ryan Mastro. Top two photos in central diamond by Adam Macchia. Bottom left photo in central diamond by Jeff Kravitz/Film Magic. Bottom right photo in central diamond by Jason Merritt/Film Magic. Bottom photo (crowd) by C. Taylor Crothers.

Library of Congress Cataloging-in-Publication Data:

Bonnaroo : what, which, this, that, the other / edited by Holly
George-Warren ; photography by Danny Clinch ... [et al.].
      p. cm.
  ISBN 978-1-4197-0256-3
1. Bonnaroo Music & Arts Festival—Pictorial works. 2. Music
festivals—Tennessee—Manchester—Pictorial works. 3. Art
festivals—Tennessee—Manchester—Pictorial works. I. George-Warren, Holly.
II. Clinch, Danny.
  ML38.M25B669 2012
  781.64'07876864--dc23

                    2011036074

Bonnaroo: What, Which, This, That, The Other © 2012 Axis Operations, LLC

Printed and bound in the United States

10 9 8 7 6 5 4 3 2 1

Abrams Image books are available at special discounts when purchased in quantity for premiums and promotions as well as fundraising or educational use. Special editions can also be created to specification. For details, contact specialsales@abramsbooks.com or the address below.

THE ART OF BOOKS SINCE 1949
115 West 18th Street
New York, NY 10011
www.abramsbooks.com

MIX
Paper from
responsible sources
FSC® C101537

Bonnaroo: What, Which, This, That, The Other was printed on Somerset Matte paper with FSC®-certified fiber. The Forest Stewardship Council® is a nonprofit entity that supports environmentally appropriate, socially beneficial, and economically viable management of the world's forests.